D0898411

RUNT

ENEMIES AREN'T ALWAYS
WHAT THEY SEEM

Runt
Written by John H. Matthews
Copyright ©2021 John H. Matthews

ISBN: 978-1-970071-22-1

Library of Congress Control Number:
2021907196

Published by Bluebullseye Press

Edited by S.C. Megale

Cover and book design
Copyright ©2021 John H. Matthews

Illustrations by Sara Willia

RUNT

ENEMIES AREN'T ALWAYS
WHAT THEY SEEM

JOHN H. MATTHEWS

bluebullseye press

To

Brennan, for

continuing to fill

your shelves with books

and your mind with imagination.

And in memory of my dad,

who never stopped

dreaming.

CHAPTER 1

It was a Wednesday when I realized I had an enemy. I don't know why that stuck out to me. Maybe I thought huge life changing events should happen on Fridays. Maybe Mondays.

The kid had everyone in school afraid of him. He'd transferred from another town after Christmas. There was a rumor that he'd punched his principal and that's why his family had to move. He was in Ms. Gonzalez's class down the hall from mine, so with the teacher's weird obsession of having us all line up and walk in alphabetical order, we weren't lined up near each other for lunch or recess. If I was walking down the hallway and saw him coming toward me, I kept my eyes down.

That strategy worked for more than three months, and three months is a lifetime in elementary school. At recess I played soccer and he didn't, but I'd see him leaning on the fence watching us several times. In the lunchroom I sat at a full table of other kids from my class and he was always off by himself in the corner, his back to everyone.

Everything was great up to that Wednesday. There were only a few weeks left in fifth grade. Next year I'd be top grade at Tall Pines Elementary. That had always confused me. There are no tall pine trees near the school. Maybe they got cut down to make room for the building?

When the first recess of the day came around, our class lined up in alphabetical order as all the classes did, placing me right in the middle. I counted 13 kids in front of me and 13 behind. I loved counting things and did it quickly, to the point that it bugged my parents. Eight bananas in the bunch Mom bought at the store. Forty-eight holes in my homemade flaxseed waffle at breakfast. Twenty-six cars crossed the road in front of us as we waited for the red light at Prosperity Lane on the way to school. Okay. I guess that is kind of annoying.

I was surprised to be in the middle of the line with the last name Noonan. Usually I was farther back because there were no kids whose last names started with X, Y, or Z, but wouldn't you know there was a Xander, a Yang, and a Zabaronick in my class.

Mrs. Baxter lined us up and we walked out of the room into the hallway. The fifth grade class across the hall always came out at the same time, which I liked, because that meant I got to walk next to Debbie Schultz, and everyone wanted to walk next to Debbie Schultz. But on that Wednesday I came around the corner into the hallway with Mr. Lee's class falling in beside ours, and it wasn't Debbie I saw.

It was him. Aaron Decker. All seven-foot tall Aaron Decker. Okay, he was really like five-foot-two, but he looked like seven feet. His shoulders were as wide as Coach Miller's, the

P.E. teacher, though admittedly Coach Miller is kind of small for a grown up. Aaron's right arm was in a cast. That was new. The tape was still bright white and fresh. No signatures from friends and classmates.

I stared straight down the hall, not looking over or making small talk like I did with Debbie. Aaron Decker. Right there beside me. In front of him was Padma Lal. Behind him was Victor Moran. How was he between them? It totally messed up the alphabet. And why was he in Mr. Lee's class now?

The lines came to the left-turn toward the playground doors. Mr. Lee was at the front and Mrs. Baxter was at the back. As soon as we made the left, I heard Aaron say something.

"Hey, runt."

I looked over at him. And as soon as I did, his left hand came out and punched my shoulder. Hard. Like two cars colliding into each other. I flew into the beige cement block wall. My feet tangled and came out from under me. The line kept moving, knowing better than to stop. Kids just stepped over my legs as I lay there on the ground. I was probably paralyzed. Or at the very least bruised.

It had been in the exact moment after going around the corner that Mr. Lee's back was to us and Mrs. Baxter couldn't see us from behind. But soon enough, the end of the line came and Mrs. Baxter was standing over me.

"What are you doing on the floor, Mo?" she said.

I looked up at her and considered telling her what happened. Then I didn't.

"I tripped."

"Get up and get to the back of the line."

I jumped up and ran to get behind Becky Zabaronick.

CHAPTER 2

Runt. That's a new one. I was used to hearing the more common ones. Shorty. Short stuff. Munchkin. Last year a sixth grader called me Bilbo Baggins. I had to look it up and was actually impressed with the effort.

But, it's true. I'm short. In a line up with the rest of fifth grade, I'm by far the most vertically challenged. I'm not taller than anyone, boys or girls. By a long shot.

I can't say I'm used to the insults, I just don't hear them that often anymore. I've grown up with most of the kids in my class, or at least gotten older. They're the ones growing. To them, I'm just Mo. Not Short Mo or Mini Mo.

During the next period while I was supposed to be writing a summary of *Wishtree*, I looked up the word runt just to see what it said. I knew the general idea, but the pictures and descriptions that came up didn't make me any happier. A runt is the smallest in a litter of animals, like puppies or kittens. And most often, the runt doesn't survive. It's just too small to fight for food and attention and just, well, dies.

I'm not from a litter of six or seven babies, though. I'm not even a twin. My brother and sister are twins but are younger than me by several years. So, I can't be a runt, right? Not by definition, at least. But I got the idea. I'm small. I'm weak. But Aaron Decker was a giant. A neanderthal of amazing proportions walking among us. He was at least four inches taller than the kid who had been the tallest in our grade, Veronica Ainsley. Her parents are both really tall, like, you see them at the store and can't stop staring at them tall, so that makes sense. My parents are both normal sized. Average, I guess.

Dad says his father was short and I must have gotten it from him. Thanks, Pawpaw.

The final bell is the only time we don't have to line up. It's a free-for-all to the door and the hallway is crazy with kids all trying to get to their buses or just out of the building to walk home, like me. I watched over my shoulder but never saw Aaron and finally relaxed as I turned onto my street, six blocks from the school.

Most days I go to my best friend's house two doors down. Felix used to be in my grade at Tall Pines but a couple years ago his mom pulled him out and started homeschooling him because he's allergic to everything. And I mean everything. Peanut butter, gluten, bees, pollen, mold, dust, and some things I never even heard of. Supposedly he has asthma, too, and carries an inhaler everywhere, but I've never seen him use it. I think he's embarrassed but I think it's kinda cool.

He hates being homeschooled but has no say in the matter. His favorite part of the day is when I get there in the afternoon and tell him everything that happened, right down to what was served for lunch and what corny joke the principal told in the morning announcements. I had to start taking notes so I didn't forget anything. One time I didn't tell him for three whole days about Coach Miller splitting his shorts open while demonstrating how to shoot a layup and I thought Felix was never going to talk to me again.

Felix was in his back yard waiting for me, already kicking the ball into his pop-up soccer goal. We practiced almost every day to get ready for tryouts. Three years earlier we'd been on a peewee soccer team together, before "the allergies." But my parents aren't into sports, or competition, or anything to do with the outdoors except for hiking to see leaves falling from trees. And Felix's parents are overprotective. I talked mine into letting me try out for the community center summer soccer league this year, and Felix had been working on permission from his.

His mouth was open the entire time I told him the very short story about my bully and being knocked to the ground. Finally he recovered a bit and the questions came fast.

"What are you gonna do? Did you push him back? Will you fight him? Are you going to change your last name so you can be at a different place in line?" Felix was out of breath with questions but still didn't grab his inhaler.

"I'm not changing my name, Felix," I said.

CHAPTER 3

Dad banged on my door. "Time to get up!"

Outside my room it was already loud. My twin brother and sister were fighting over something—they were always fighting over something—and Mom was trying to settle the argument in her usual peaceful voice. It never worked.

Mom and Dad said they were hippies at heart, that they were both born in what was called the Summer of Love and even though they missed the actual era of the hippies, it was in their blood. I had no idea what any of that meant so I looked it up on my computer once. The pictures

I found of hippies looked nothing like my parents. My mom drove a Volvo and Dad was an orthodontist. They both had peace sign stickers on their cars and listened to horrible music with lots of humming and tambourines. Dad was always playing guitar and Mom kept telling him he should perform at an open mic night at the coffee shop near the mall. He'd say he's not good enough but I could tell he wanted to.

They were older than any other parents in my grade. By a lot. But they pretended to be young. It didn't work well. Dad had T-shirts from when he was in college with names like Crosby, Stills, Nash & Young, and Joni Mitchell.

I was their first child and they named me Moon, which I feel is probably the worst name you can give a kid. Outside the house I go by Mo, but they refuse to call me that and stick with Moon. The twins are Janis and Ian, which just makes me hate my name even more because they got normal sounding ones. Each school year I try to talk to my teachers before the first class and tell them I go by Mo, not Moon, and every one of them has completely understood and never called me Moon once. I'm serious. Even my first grade art teacher Mr. Cornell, and he actually does look like the pictures I found of hippies.

Downstairs Janis and Ian were fighting over a box of cereal while Dad scribbled in a notebook he'd been carrying everywhere. I considered telling him about my bully, but knew he would just tell me something about embracing him and being friends.

"Where's Mom?"

"She got called to substitute today," he said. "She left a few minutes ago."

I froze. That was not good.

"Which school?"

He didn't look up. The sounds from the twins blocked everything out.

"Dad, which school is Mom at today?"

"Hmm? Oh. I'm not sure," he said. "Maybe you'll finally be lucky and have her in your class."

Lucky. Right.

"Are you riding the bus this morning?" He said.

"With the twins?" I said. "That's a hard no."

My stomach was wrenched up the entire walk to school. Thirty-eight times she'd been a substitute at my school and not once in my class. The odds were heavily against me. I just had to get through fifth and sixth grades and go off to middle school. She only subbed for elementary classes, so I'd be safe then.

Did Mrs. Baxter look sick yesterday? I think she sneezed once, but it was during recess and she said her allergies were bothering her.

I was so distracted worrying about having Mom as a substitute that I didn't see Aaron Decker until I was walking right past him. He was standing looking in the open passenger door of a big SUV. As I went by I heard a man's voice speaking loudly, but I was watching the giant boy while at the same time trying to avoid him, so I didn't hear what was being said.

Approaching the building, my thoughts were going away from him and back to the whole Mom-the-substitute-teacher-crisis. As I reached for the door handle, I saw myself reflected in the glass and over my head the dark silhouette of another kid. I recognized his black hoodie immediately. He was right behind me. My pulse soared and sweat formed on my forehead in that split second. Before I could react, two hands struck my back and I flew forward. My face slammed into the glass and left a smeared drool print down to where I landed.

"Out of my way, runt."

He was gone by the time I could turn around, having slipped in through one of the other open doors.

My nose hurt and I reached up to rub it as I walked into the building. My hand came away with a bright red flood of blood just as I heard the first kids around me reacting.

A string of words floated past me, "Gross!" and "Get away from me!" and my personal favorite, "His nose is bleeding!" Brilliant observation.

Not knowing what to do, I just stopped in the middle of the lobby. I was getting bounced around like a pinball as another busload of kids unloaded and barged in to get to their classes. Meanwhile, the blood wasn't stopping. I tried to move toward the wall, to some sort of relative safety, when a hand landed on my shoulder and I jumped, expecting to be thrown to the floor.

"Mo, are you okay?"

I turned around. It was Coach Miller and I felt a small bit of relief. He led me through the crowd and down the hall to the nurse's office.

CHAPTER 4

"What happened to you?" Nurse Pettie had worked at the school for twenty years. Last year, they threw her a celebration in the lunchroom. She was so surprised that she cried.

I wanted to tell her what happened. I really did. But I didn't.

"I tripped and fell into the front door."

"It's okay, Mo. We'll fix you right up," she said.

It was another thirty minutes before she cleared me to go to class. First bell had rung long before and the halls were empty. By some strange fate, I'd worn a red shirt with our school mascot on it. A panther. A little drop of blood had dried on the black part, but right where the cat's eye would be. We had played two hands of Uno while the gauze sticks were taped to my upper lip to catch any blood. She gave me alcohol wipes to clean my face and declared me "good as new."

I took the long way through the school to my room. The walls were filled with artwork and projects in the lower grades. Passing the kindergarten classes there were crayon self portraits, the kids imagining themselves as everything from basketball players to astronauts. One appeared to draw himself as a spider. I scanned the walls outside the first graders' rooms where Janis and Ian were, in separate classes because no teacher would want to deal with them together.

Their art projects seemed to be about something they loved. There were drawings of footballs, candy, and a Christmas tree. One kid had drawn the front of the school. Looking for bonus points there.

On one wall, I found a toilet paper roll glued to green construction paper with brown lines coming out of the roll. I hope that the teacher didn't ask Ian what it was because I'm pretty sure it was supposed to be the pipe coming out of the toilet. He'd been asking about plumbing for months. For some reason he thought it all just went out into the yard. On the other side of the hall I saw Janis' jet black horse painting, which made sense because everything in her room was horses. That girl was obsessed.

I was just about to open the door to my classroom when I saw the small sign on the wall, MRS. BAXTER and under it FIFTH GRADE. Right then all my anxiety about having my mom as a substitute returned and I hoped that my nose would start bleeding again and I could spend the day playing card games with Nurse Pettie.

I jumped when the door opened and Mrs. Baxter was standing there. I'd never been happier to see her.

"Are you coming in, Mo?"

"Yes," I said. "Yes, ma'am."

I handed her the nurse's note and went to my desk.

Everyone had their math books out and a bunch of fractions were written on the dry erase board. I grabbed my book and paper and tried to catch up, all the while thanking any one or thing I could think of that Mom was not teaching my class. It was the first thing that had gone right that day.

I watched the clock as it ticked closer to recess, now able to think about Aaron Decker again. Maybe he'd gotten his bullying out of the way early and wouldn't do anything else. I knew that was ridiculous to think, but I had to hope. The three chiming bells sounded from the speakers and once Mrs. Baxter told us to, we all stood and formed our line.

Here it came. Should I defend myself this time? Or just try to jump out of the way if he tried to push me? What if I moved just enough that his shove missed me and *he* went falling to the floor? I would be the hero of fifth grade. The giant slayer.

We started moving and my stomach tightened with every step closer to the door. With the angle, I couldn't even see the hallway until I made the left turn out of the room.

Four people ahead of me, then three, two. I

made the left and stepped forward into the hallway and came to a complete stop so fast that Hannah Petersen bumped into me as I looked across the hall.

We locked eyes.

Everything around me blurred and my head started swimming. But it wasn't Aaron Decker.

"Mom?"

CHAPTER 5

"There you are, Moon!" my mother said.

I'm pretty sure I died, like right there. My racing pulse stopped and I got sweaty all over. Or maybe I just hoped I'd died. Because my mom was six feet away from me and calling me Moon in front of two entire fifth grade classes. She kept talking but I didn't hear anything she said.

Finally I was able to take in a deep breath and by then we were halfway down the hall to the playground doors and I didn't even remember taking any steps. And that's when I realized he was right there beside me, staring at me with a huge, evil grin.

"Hey, Moooooon." He dragged Moon out like it had twenty O's in it.

I wanted to be home, or in the nurse's office, or back in first grade with Janis and Ian making pictures of myself as an airline pilot or a rodeo clown.

Out on the playground, Aaron disappeared off to the other side and I relaxed a bit. Maybe he realized that there were too many teachers to try anything. Mom was out there standing with Mrs. Baxter and the other fifth grade teachers, talking and laughing. She saw me looking and waved, then turned to the other teachers and pointed at me, probably telling some super embarrassing story about when I used to run around the house in my underwear singing "This Land is Your Land."

I wanted to hide. I wanted to be invisible.

By the time I looked around for something to do—soccer on the small dirt area, speed climbing the monkey bars, or having races on the far side of the playground—it was time to go in. Lines formed and another class was between mine and Aaron's, so it was an uneventful walk back to class.

At my desk I took out my history book, flipped to the pages written on the board, and started to read. To my left I heard whispering, a dangerous thing to do in Mrs. Baxter's class. She was a legend at Tall Pines when it came to discipline. Rumor has it that a few years ago she made a girl stand in the corner for an entire day just because she giggled when Mrs. Baxter said Uranus during the science lesson.

The whispering continued and I looked over to see Jimmy Foster and Ravi Parekh looking at me. And it wasn't just them. As I scanned the room, eyes kept turning to me then darting away.

I realized it had happened.

The five years I spent keeping kids from knowing my real name had come to an end. A screeching halt. Maybe I can be home schooled by Felix's mom or just skip the rest of school and go work somewhere. I tried to concentrate on my book, but the chapter on the fall of Rome didn't keep my attention from the more immediate dangers.

The bell for lunch rang and I didn't move. The whole class was lined up and waiting for me to take my place in the middle when it began.

"Come on, Moon."

"Hey Moon, we're hungry."

"Hey moon boy, get moving."

After all these years of acting like I hated it, after hiding it, I don't know how it happened. I felt the words come up from my gut and couldn't stop them. I stood so fast that my chair fell with a crash behind me and I turned to the line of kids and yelled. I yelled louder than I'd ever yelled

before. Louder than the twins yell when they couldn't watch TV. Louder than Coach Miller laughed when a kid farted in P.E. while doing push ups.

"YES! My name is Moon. Moon Noonan. Get over it. It's my name and I like it, so if you don't, then you can go—"

I don't really know what else I said, but I went on a while longer and I'm pretty sure it was bad. Twenty-six kids and Mrs. Baxter stood there staring at me, jaws dropped.

When I finished, the room was quiet. Even the hallway outside the room was silent. It was that Saturday morning lying in bed before anyone else woke up quiet.

Eerie quiet.

Then I saw my mom standing in the door. But her jaw wasn't dropped. She didn't look angry or shocked.

She was smiling.

CHAPTER 6

The halls were empty by the time Mrs. Baxter handed me a note and told me to go to the office. Every other kid on this side of the school— fourth, fifth and sixth graders—were in the lunchroom eating square pizza. There was always pizza on Fridays and I was missing it. Felix liked me to describe the pizza since he can't eat it anymore because of something in the crust. His mom made some version of it that he said tastes like old newspapers. I don't know how he knew what old newspapers tasted like.

I'd only been sent to the office once in my time

at Tall Pines Elementary, and that was because
I had been late to class because of a line in the
bathroom in second grade. I really had to go so
I waited and waited. The assistant principal had
sent a note back to my teacher. I wasn't supposed
to look at it but I snuck a peak. It just said,
"Lighten up, the kid had to pee."

I pushed the heavy glass door to the office.
Three women at desks stopped what they were
doing and looked up at me. The nearest one
spoke.

"Can I help you?"

I handed her the note Mrs. Baxter gave me.
She read it and nodded.

"Okay, Mr. Noonan." That's when you know
you're in trouble, when grownups start calling
you mister. "Have a seat with Mr. Decker."

I felt like I needed Felix's inhaler. "What?"

She pointed behind me. "Sit."

I turned. There he was, sitting in one of the
only two chairs. I looked back at the woman, who
offered no other suggestions to my blank stare.

"Please sit. Mrs. Baxter will be here soon and
you'll meet with the principal."

That didn't even scare me anymore. Send me straight to the principal. Please. I'd rather be in there. But instead I'm sitting in a hard metal chair next to the kid who made the last week horrible.

Our arms bumped but the chairs were connected so there was no way to scoot away from him. He didn't say anything, but he didn't pull his arm away, either. He just sat there staring at nothing.

The clock on the wall didn't move. The second hand was stuck in that perpetual motion about twelve seconds away from the top, making a little jump up and returning right back to where it had been. If the hour and minute hands were correct then I completely missed pizza, not that I could have eaten any as nauseous as I felt.

The door opened and Mom walked in. She looked over at me but showed no sign of support. No smile like before. I'd have welcomed a "Hi, Moon," right then, but my brief moment of joy in seeing her was quickly replaced when I realized that the boy who was now my mortal enemy had been sent to the office by my own mother. She stopped and talked to the woman at the first desk, who made a call, then stood.

"Aaron, please come this way."

The three of them disappeared down a hall around the corner, back to where the row of offices were, starting with the nurse's station, the assistant principal, then the principal, Mrs. Juliano. Past that is a large room where the school counselor worked when she wasn't visiting classrooms. I'd only been in her office once. There's bright green carpet like a football field, colorful pictures on the walls, and bean bag chairs. It was a grownup's idea of what they thought kids liked.

I wondered for the first time what Aaron did to get sent to the office, especially with my mom teaching his class. At home we got away with about everything and she never got mad. I guess that's part of her being a hippie. But at least I was delayed in going to the principal's office until they were done, then I'd get to see Aaron after he'd been talked to for whatever reason he was in the office. Maybe he'd be crying.

Mrs. Baxter came in and the woman at the desk

made a call and just like before stood and asked me to follow. Mom and Aaron hadn't come back yet, which confused me. How could we be going to the principal's office if they were in there? We went around the corner, passed the nurses station and the assistant principal's office. The woman from the desk stopped and opened the principal's door and stepped back for us to walk in. As I did I looked left down the hall and saw the counselor's door closed. It was never closed.

CHAPTER 7

I was in no hurry after school. The last bus had pulled away before I even walked out the door. In my backpack was a note from the principal for my parents, but I'm sure Mom talked to someone before leaving.

From what I heard, the assistant principal took Mrs. Baxter's class while she was gone for an hour, and gave a surprise spelling test with random words he chose from a dictionary. None of them were from our list for the week. I'm sure the whole class was thrilled with me for that.

When afternoon recess came I didn't feel like

playing anything. I sat on the ground leaning on the chain link fence that separated the playground from someone's back yard. This was the farthest possible spot I could be from my mom and the other teachers. I didn't see Aaron anywhere.

The rest of the afternoon went by in a haze. I barely listened to anything Mrs. Baxter said and mostly tried to think of ways to never come back to school. So far, fifth grade was no fun and I wanted nothing to do with it.

I got to Felix's house and found him in his room reading. He got excited when I walked in and began pelting me with questions as always, then stopped and looked at me.

"What's wrong?" he said.

"Huh?"

"Something's wrong."

"How can you tell?"

"I just can," he said. "We've been best friends since preschool. Is it the bully? What did he do?"

I'd forgotten about the bloody nose that morning. It seemed like weeks had passed with everything else that happened. I started from the beginning and left nothing out. When

Felix wanted a snack he wouldn't even let me stop talking. I just followed him through the house and kept telling him the events of the day while he made two almond butter sandwiches. We were back up in his room and I was talking through the sandwich in my mouth when I finally finished the story.

"Man. I wish I was back in school," he said.

"Seriously? That's what you get from the story?" I said. "It's horrible. Just horrible."

He shook his head. "Mo. Get real. I spend all-day-every-day with my mom. Five hours of it is with her as my teacher. I get no recess, no P.E., and no free reading time until after she's 'dismissed' me for the day."

"That does sound pretty bad," I said. "Is she gonna let you try out tomorrow? She promised you could in fifth grade."

"Not sure yet," Felix said. "I'm hoping so. I'm going to get ready as if we're going. If Dad has any say in it I will."

"You better be there."

"I'll try."

The phone rang downstairs and I knew it was

Mom calling from home. I grabbed my bag.

"Nine o'clock," I said.

"I'm gonna try."

"There is no try…" I said in my best Yoda voice.

"Only do." Felix replied in his.

I didn't know what to expect when I got home. The twins were upstairs screaming at each other and Mom was in the kitchen putting a vegan lasagna into the oven. We aren't even vegan. I held the envelope out for her and waited. After washing her hands she stepped over to me, took the envelope, and sat it down on the counter without opening it.

She wrapped her arms around me in a tight hug. "What happened with Mrs. Juliano?"

"They talked to me about some of the words I used," I said. "I don't even remember saying them."

"You were pretty mad."

"It's been a rough week."

"Really? What else is going on?"

I'd kept it to myself, well, myself and Felix, long enough.

"I'm getting bullied." It felt different saying it to my mom. It made it more real. More serious.

Talking with Felix everything can be exaggerated to the point it is almost silly. But once I said it to Mom, it became something else.

She took my hand and led me to the living room where we sat down on the couch.

"Tell me."

So I did. From the beginning. Everything Aaron Decker had done and that I was afraid he would do. She listened, holding my hand the entire time. A couple times I thought I might cry but was able to hold it back. When I finished, she hugged me again, then ran her hand through my hair.

"I'm so sorry you're going through this."

I nodded and stared at my hands.

"Aaron Decker?" she said. "The boy that was in the office with you?"

"Yeah."

"Do you think maybe you can talk to him? Try to be his friend?"

That was exactly what I expected from my hippie mother. Love everyone. Peace and understanding. Blah, blah, blah, while you're getting bloody noses and shoved to the floor.

"Mom, he doesn't like me, why would I do that?"

"Just… try," she said. "For me?"

"Why was he in the office? What did he do?"

"You know I can't tell you that," she said. "Just try to be friendly. You might be surprised."

"It's scary."

"Everyone should have a friend," she said.

CHAPTER 8

I was so eager for tryouts that I was dressed and had breakfast two hours before they began. Dad reluctantly agreed to take me early and the field was empty except for two guys setting up cones for the drills. We kicked my ball around on the side of the field for another half hour before any other kids showed up. I kept expecting him to bring up the note from the principal or Aaron Decker or anything from the day before, but he didn't. He just kicked the ball with me and talked about whatever I wanted. Which was anything but those things.

More kids arrived, most in the green and white colors of the town soccer team, the Hornets. I recognized most of them; some I didn't. Two boys from my school got there and we started kicking together. Dad went and sat on the bleachers, his notebook and pen out.

No sign of Felix. If he was coming, he'd have been early.

A black SUV pulled up and the back door opened. Then Aaron Decker got out. This can't be happening. I thought about leaving. It isn't worth it. It's only soccer. I can play in my back yard. I've heard chess club is fun. I can try that instead. But I know that I can't leave. I've looked forward to this all year. My whole life. Community soccer. A real, organized soccer team run by coaches, not volunteer dads that would rather be anywhere else or are way too into it and yell at you like crazy.

Whistles were blown and we lined up. I watched Aaron and moved to the other end of the line from him. There were twenty-eight of us trying out. The coach went down the line and assigned us numbers: one, two, three, four, then started over with one, two, three, four again. When he was done he told all the ones to go to the far corner, twos to the opposite corner, and so on. When he blew the whistle, we all ran to where we were supposed to be.

I was a three and went to the near corner of the field. In the mess of eleven and twelve year old boys I lost sight of Aaron. He wasn't in my line and I couldn't see him in any of the other groups.

We stood there waiting for the coach. I leaned down to adjust my shin guards and glanced left and right.

Ten legs. Ten legs is five boys. Plus me.

There's only six in my line. But I counted twenty-eight total. There should be one more. Then I felt someone come up from behind and stand beside me. I didn't want to look over because I knew who it was even though I hoped I was wrong.

The coaches were talking in the middle of the field and I heard Mom's voice in my head. I squeezed my eyes shut as hard as I could, and said to myself, "*You can do this, Mo. He's just a kid like you."* Then I turned to my right, stuck my hand out, and talked.

"I'm Mo. I don't know why you've been pushing me but I'd like you to stop. Maybe we can be friends instead?"

My hand hung in the air waiting for a shake that never came. He turned and looked at me, eyes moving up and down, judging me. His mouth opened and Aaron Decker was about to speak. Would he just call me runt again and shove me? But the voice that came was not his.

"Okay, boys. Here's the first drill." The coach barked his orders to have us dribble our soccer balls through the cones then back around to the start again.

We turned and ran, balls falling to the ground and being batted left and right by the insides of shoes. Aaron was behind me and I kept wanting to speed up, stay out of his reach in case he tried to push me again.

The next hour was spent running, dribbling, kicking and doing any type of drill imaginable. I was exhausted and my legs were getting wobbly. But my thoughts were on Aaron and what he was about to say. I don't even know if I did any of the drills correctly. I did get the ball into the goal a few times when they had us shooting free kicks, and barely noticed the cheers from behind me.

One last line up of the whole group. Aaron was nine down from me. A pep talk and how not to be disappointed if we didn't make a team. I kept looking down the line. What was he going to say? Should I catch him after try outs to talk to him again?

The whistle blew and kids went everywhere. Parents came onto the field carrying their fold up camping chairs and found their children, hugs and pats on backs and words of encouragement and praising how well they did.

Then I saw Aaron. He was walking alone out to the parking lot as the black SUV that dropped him off pulled up.

CHAPTER 9

"Where were you?" I was on the phone with Felix as soon as we got home, even though I knew what happened.

"Mom changed her mind," he said. "She read a story about some kid getting a concussion playing soccer and said I couldn't go."

"I needed you there, man. Aaron Decker tried out!"

"What!"

"I know. What if he gets on my team?" I said. "If I make a team, that is."

"You're gonna make a team. I just know it," Felix said.

"I don't even care which one at this point. I'll take the lowest team with the nose pickers," I said. The nose pickers were the least skilled. The ones who were there because their parents wanted to see them in a uniform on a field, but who had no interest in the game. They pretty much just stood there on the grass, well, picking their noses.

"You're better than that," Felix said.

"I can come over to play after lunch," I said.

There was a longer silence than I was used to before he spoke again.

"I'm actually going on a play date," Felix said. "Well, my mom calls it a play date."

I felt like Aaron Decker just punched me again.

"A play date? With who?"

"It's a group of homeschooled kids. My mom found them online and thought it would be good if I hung out with them," Felix said. "I don't want to. Please, believe me."

"I believe you."

After we hung up, I lay down on my bed and stared at the white ceiling. It felt like I'd just lost my best friend, even though I knew that was silly.

He was just going to play with a bunch of other kids I didn't know. It wasn't like he was going to like one of them better than me. Was he? Nah.

Through the walls I heard Dad playing acoustic guitar. He might have actually gotten a little better.

CHAPTER 10

I woke up to the smell of something cooking downstairs. I wasn't quite sure what. Once I got to the kitchen I found out it was almond milk flax seed pancakes with fresh honey from the farmer's market. Just once I'd love some real maple syrup. And some real pancakes.

"What are you doing for the science fair?" Mom said.

My fork stopped halfway up to my mouth. The science fair. I recalled Mrs. Baxter talking about it at one point.

"I'm working on it," I said. "When is it again?"

"Next Saturday," Mom said.

"Like, a whole week away?"

"Well, today is Sunday, so six days," she said. "What's your project going to be?"

Awkward. I had no ideas for the science fair. I remember Mrs. Baxter said no volcanoes or anything that blows up. That severely limited my options. The project would count toward a quarter of my grade for science for the whole year.

Dad was reading the newspaper across the table. I saw some big words on the front about an earthquake.

"I was thinking about making one of those things that tells you about how strong an earthquake is," I said. I didn't even know what it was called much less how to make one.

The newspaper folded down quickly and I saw Dad's face light up.

"A seismograph?" He sounded excited.

"Is that what it's called?" I said.

"It is."

"Then that." I needed to figure out how to spell it so I could go search for them online.

"That sounds like a great idea, Moon," Dad said. "I had an idea once on how to make one. You need to—"

"Honey, this is Moon's science project, not yours," Mom said.

"It's okay, Mom. I'd love Dad's help."

"No. You need to do this yourself."

Dang. I thought I had the easy way out there.

"But I can—" Dad started.

"No," Mom said.

Looked like I was on my own. Six days to build a seismograph.

The twins were covered in honey and flax seed pancakes were all over the table. Mom just looked at them and smiled. I ate half a pancake then asked to be excused.

I turned on the school computer in my room and started searching for seismographs. I called Felix while scrolling through pictures of huge, complicated looking metal boxes with a needle that bounced around and drew lines on paper with graphs all over it.

"Hey, Mo." Felix took the phone from his mom who answered.

"What do you know about seismographs?" I said.

"Seismometers measure the strength of an earthquake," he said.

"Right. But how do you build one?"

"Ohhh." Felix knew exactly what was happening. "How long until the science fair?"

"Six days."

There was quiet on the other end of the line.

"Felix?"

"Yeah. That's not a lotta time," Felix said.

"Tell me something I don't know."

"When did you pick your project?" he said.

"About five minutes ago."

"Sounds about right." Felix laughed. "A basic seismometer shouldn't be too hard to make. It won't look or work anything like the big fancy ones you'll find searching online, though."

"I just need it to look like it works," I said.

"You can do that." Felix tried to cheer me up, but the tone of his voice wasn't reassuring.

By the time I got off the phone with Felix, I had a plan. Or the beginning of a plan, at least. Pretty much I had a shopping list. That was it.

CHAPTER 11

My stomach grew tighter with every step toward school. And it wasn't the second bowl of homemade shredded wheat Mom made me eat. I was thinking about Aaron.

Another week of worrying about being punched, pushed, bloodied, murdered, or worse.

I made it into the building and to Mrs. Baxter's room safely. No sign of him. At first recess I held my breath lining up in the hall, but Debbie Schultz was beside me again. I couldn't even relax enough to make my usual small talk with her. She smiled and said hi to me and I'm not even sure I responded.

My head was swiveling back and forth, forward and backward, watching for him. Maybe he'd been moved to yet another fifth grade class or joined the Army or something. There was only one class left he hadn't been in, other than mine, and that would be the worst.

All clear on the playground. I played a distracted game of kickball. Back through the hall and into my classroom again with no bodily injury. That's a win in my book.

"Time for science." Mrs. Baxter turned on the overhead projector with the list of everyone's names and what their project was going to be beside it. Only three didn't have anything in the second column.

"Becky?" Mrs. Baxter said. "Have you chosen your science fair project?"

"Yes, ma'am," Becky said.

I got nervous. What if someone else took my idea? I scanned the list on the screen and nobody had any version of seismograph or seismometer, but there were two others who hadn't said.

"And what is it, Becky?" Mrs. Baxter said.

I was staring at Becky Zabaronick, waiting to hear her answer.

"I'm growing three different sets of grass seed, treating each one differently."

"How so?" Mrs. Baxter said.

"One will have had weed killer applied to the soil. One will have no weed killer. The third will have no weed killer and I am talking to it every day."

"Talking to the grass?" Mrs. Baxter said.

"Yes, ma'am."

"Very good." Mrs. Baxter took her marker and wrote *Grass growing experiment* next to Becky's name. "Who is next?"

I rose my hand quickly. I never raise my hand, much less quickly. But I didn't want to be the last person in case they said my idea first.

"Okay, Mo. What is your project?"

"I'm building a seismonitor," I said.

"Do you mean a seismometer?" Mrs. Baxter said.

I heard chuckles from the class even though most of them didn't know the difference. Fifth graders just revel in the failure of others.

"Yes, ma'am," I said. "A seismometer. Sorry."

"Have you started building it yet?" she said.

I haven't but can't say that with five days to go.

"I've been drawing out my plans and am starting construction tonight."

"Excellent," Mrs. Baxter said. "It would be a bonus to your project to display your drawings and plans on your board to show how you developed it."

"Yes, thank you," I said. "I was planning on that."

I was planning on that? I hadn't even drawn anything yet. Now I have to build it and draw pictures of what I built. This just keeps getting better.

CHAPTER 12

I walked past my street after school toward the hardware store a few blocks away. I had my shopping list from Felix and $20 Mom gave me for supplies. "No candy," she'd said.

The hardware store always felt like another world. It was full of things I had no idea how to use, and had that smell of fresh wood, which I enjoyed. Dad would come here almost every Saturday morning to buy something for a weekend project. Most of the times the project never got finished, or even started. We had boxes in the garage full of light switches, water sprinklers, paint cans and brushes, and a lot of other things. He usually made me come with him so I could "learn" about working on the house. So far I've only learned how to buy things then do nothing with them.

"Good afternoon, Mo!" Mr. Kaplan said as I walked through the electric sliding door. He owned the store and helped everyone. He's good at "upselling," Dad said. I'm guessing that is why the boxes in the garage are so full. "What can I help you with today?"

I looked at the list in my hand, then offered it to him. He read through it as if it were the elements of some great structure, nodding the entire time.

"Yup. We have all this," he said. "But what do you mean by a weight? There's several different things we can use for that. What are you building?"

I explained the seismometer to him and how the weight needed to hang down from the fishing line with a pencil attached to the end so it would mark on the paper. He looked out toward the aisles of white shelves while his finger tapped the list.

"I think I have exactly what you need," he said.

I followed him through the store as he pushed a small shopping cart. The container of plaster of Paris looked like a milk jug but weighed a lot more. He said it was a powder that you add water to and it gets really hard, like cement, but easier to use. Then he gathered a few pieces of stray wood from the scrap pile, sized them up against each other, and put them in the cart.

"I won't even charge you for the wood," he said.

Next was fishing line. Then a cat litter box. After that he showed me small electric motors for hobbyists. He said one of the smallest ones would turn slowly with a pair of AA batteries attached to it. It went in the cart.

"Now, for your weight," he said. We were on an aisle with tools like I'd never seen before. He handed me a small piece of metal that was a lot heavier than it looked like it should be. "This is called a plumb. Carpenters use them to mark perfect vertical lines."

It was shiny and brass colored, with a black tip. The metal was cold to my hand. I liked the feel of it. I rubbed the sharp point with my finger, but it didn't leave a mark.

"How can I make it write?" I said.

Mr. Kaplan raised a finger in the air like I imagined an inventor would do when they had a great idea.

I handed the plumb back to him. He twisted

the black tip and it unscrewed off the rest of the metal. An aisle over, he picked up a short pencil like you use for mini-golf. Wouldn't you know it, the pencil slid right up into the hole.

"I think you'd want to cut the pencil down a bit where only about maybe half-an-inch is showing, so your weight stays at the bottom of the fishing line. Then you can fix the pencil in there with hot glue."

It was genius. He had the same look in his eyes that Dad did when I told him I was building a seismograph. And Mom didn't even need to know I had help from a grown up.

We gathered the remaining things and he pushed the cart to the front counter and unloaded everything. I hadn't been looking at prices and started to worry.

"I only have $20, Mr. Kaplan."

He looked at all the items and scanned them, watching the total price on screen go up. It was at $20.86 when he finished.

"Hmm," he said. "Seems that since you don't need the metal tip to the plumb, you shouldn't pay full price for that."

With a couple of buttons pressed, the total came down to $19.94. I handed him the $20 that had been crumpled in my pocket all day. When he handed me the six cents, I dropped them in the 'Take a Penny, Leave a Penny' cup, and Mr. Kaplan smiled.

I thanked him and headed toward the door with my heavy bag, wishing I'd ridden my bike instead of walking.

"Oh, Mo." Mr. Kaplan came up behind me out front beside the lawn mowers lined up for sale.

He handed me a white roll of paper like he used in the cash registers.

"I think this would work well for you," he said.

"I don't have any money left."

"My donation, as long as you bring the finished project by for me to see," he said. "Good luck at the science fair!"

CHAPTER 13

I stared at the items I had purchased the day before. They were spread out on Dad's workbench in the garage as I'd seen him do with so many projects. Mine couldn't end up in the box in the corner, though.

Every few minutes the door to the hallway would open. Dad's head would poke around the edge and ask if I was doing okay, then I'd hear Mom yell from somewhere else in the house to leave me alone.

Pacing myself, with four more weeknights to work, I started on the structure. I found nails in a drawer and a hammer. Twice I ran up to my room and called Felix for his advice.

Usually I'm not allowed to use Dad's tools without his help. Especially the hammer. He said if you're not careful with it, you could really hurt yourself. But once, when he was putting together some shelves for the laundry room, he hit his own finger with the hammer. It was bruised and swollen for days.

While building, I saw a flaw in the design. The bar that stuck out to hold the weight over the paper would move too much. I stared at the drawing I'd made with Felix's help and added two extra lines, an upside down V running from either side of the end of the bar. Happy with my idea, I found two pieces of wood that would work.

It was weird, but I was enjoying myself. Who knew I liked science? But putting things together to build something that wasn't from a box was fun. I loved LEGO as much as any kid when I was little, and to be honest, I still play with them sometimes. Though now I usually build a tall tower then take a slow motion video of knocking it down with a football. Seeing all the different colored bricks fly around is like making my own little action movie.

By the time Mom had dinner done, I was happy with my progress. I wanted to go back out to the garage afterwards, but she said it was time to shower and relax before bed.

CHAPTER 14

After school on Friday I went straight home to finish up my science fair project. Nothing like last minute. I only stopped for dinner, then was back in the garage. It was almost my bedtime and I was still working on the electric motor and getting frustrated when Mom asked me to come to the kitchen. I was glad to take a break from wiring up the batteries.

"Moon," she said.

"Mom," I said.

"I have something to tell you." She got quiet but was smiling really big.

Dad was standing there, too, also smiling.

"No," I said. "You're not having another baby, are you?"

That would be it, the end of having my own room. The twins had shared a room since they were born, but soon one of them would take the last remaining bedroom. Another kid meant someone had to share, and it wasn't going to be me.

"No, Moon. It's not that. Goodness no, it's not that," Dad said.

Mom looked over at him with one of those looks that I knew he'd said something he shouldn't have.

"You made the team," Mom said.

"What?"

"The soccer team," she said. "I just got an email from the coach."

I made the soccer team? An actual team with an actual coach?

"First practice is next week," she said. "We need to go buy your uniform on Sunday."

Visions of long runs down the field came to my head, the ball floating off my feet, defenders falling off to the sides, unable to keep up with me or take the ball. With the flick of a foot, I send it flying, just over two heads, then it arcs down and passes through the keeper's hopeful hands into the goal.

"That's great, son." Dad gave me a hug while patting my back a little too hard at the same time.

Soccer team. Then I thought of the three different levels of teams. I was happy to be chosen, definitely, but still, I didn't want to be with the nose pickers.

"Which one?" I said. "Which team?"

They are divided by color. The league colors are green and white. The top level team, the best players, are the green team. The next level is the white team. Then the lowest, the nose pickers, are the grey team.

"Let me see. I think it said somewhere." She stared at her phone while scrolling with the tip of her finger. "The white team."

The weight of a thousand soccer balls left my stomach. The white team. It was all I could ask or hope for. The players who made green team are the best and have been playing several years already. Something about my tryout earned me a spot on the white team. But the feeling of dread swept over me quickly again.

"Do you know who else made the white team?" I said.

"I don't. The email doesn't have a list of everyone," she said. "But you'll find out next week at practice."

I tried to not let the worry about possibly being on a team with Aaron Decker bother me and went back to the garage. I only had that night for finishing touches.

And to actually make the thing work.

CHAPTER 15

Dad pulled the station wagon up to the front curb of the school. Other kids were unloading their projects and I immediately got nervous. I stayed up way past my bedtime working and was tired and a bit grumpy. I hadn't even had time to call Felix to tell him about making the soccer team since I found out so late.

I saw Darius Evans from Ms. Gonzales' class carrying a windmill that was taller than him, like the huge white ones you see out in the ocean or in pictures of Hawaii. His mom was an engineer and definitely helped him. It looked perfect.

Becky Zabaronick was pushing a cart with several clay pots on it. I only saw grass growing from one of them.

I had a box over the top of mine. I didn't want to be judged by everyone before I even set it up, plus I was afraid parts would fall off and I'd lose them.

I walked into the school gym and the combined smell of sweat and vinegar hit my nose. I was used to the sweat smell. It was always like that in the gym. But how many kids were using vinegar in their projects?

My table was in the middle of the room. Ten rows and eight columns, plus four more tables in an eleventh row. Eighty-four kids. Eighty-four projects. And this was just fifth grade. If you won here, each of the grade winners would compete against each other for best project at Tall Pines Elementary at a special assembly next week. A sixth grader always won. It just made sense. They're older and had done more science fairs.

I could tell that the tables were assigned randomly. Only six people from my class were near me. Becky was at the next table trying to make her three clay pots take up more room than they really did. The board she stood up behind them just had pictures of grass on it.

Debbie Schultz had her project set up a few tables away. It looked like something about rocket engines. Cool. She saw me and looked like she was about to walk over when my dad found me. He'd carried my board in and unfolded it on the table behind my box.

"I'm proud of you, Moon," he said.

"I haven't won anything."

"I know. I'm just proud of you. You did this all by yourself."

He hadn't even seen the finished project yet, so he might change his mind on the whole proud thing. I didn't tell him about all the advice Felix had given me. Or how Mr. Kaplan had hand picked everything.

"Thanks, Dad," I said. I wasn't fast enough to move out of the way and he put his arms around me and gave me a tight hug. Right there in front of everyone.

It was then that Aaron Decker walked up. He had a paper shopping bag. I saw him just staring at us hugging and I pulled away from my dad.

Aaron turned to the table across from mine and pulled small boxes out of the shopping bag and lined them up. He had a note card for each box. I couldn't read what was written on them and didn't want him to know I was interested.

"You want to introduce me to any of your friends?" Dad said.

"Not really."

"Okay. Maybe later," he said.

"When's Mom coming?" I said.

He looked at his watch. "She'll bring the littles closer to two o'clock." That's what they called Janis and Ian. The littles. I don't know if they ever called me the big, since I'm not.

Dad saw the mom of one of his patients and walked over to talk to her. Aaron was done setting up and wandered off. I stepped over to look at his table. The boxes were maybe two-inches square with lids on them. The notecards had long names that were hard to read, but underneath each name was what looked more like English. Beetle. Cockroach. Butterfly.

Of course Aaron Decker had a bug collection.

CHAPTER 16

Mom showed up with the twins just as judging began. They were all sitting in the stands with the other families, while the kids had to talk to the judges alone, explain our project, and demonstrate it if needed.

I saw the blades of the wind turbine spinning a couple rows over.

A drone flew up into the air. It hit the ceiling and fell back down, crashing into a terrarium with three snakes in it.

Finally the judges were on my row. They listened to Becky talk about her project. Turned out the only pot with any grass in it was the one she'd put weed killer on. The other two had both died.

The two judges then went to Aaron Decker's table across from me. One of them was Mrs. Ehrlman, the sixth grade science teacher. The other was Mr. Monroe, from East Branch Middle School, where I'd go in two years.

I moved to where I could see what Aaron did, and hear him speak. Up to then I'd heard nothing more than one or two grunted words at a time from him.

I was impressed at how he talked about the insects, described their habits and what they ate. He actually knew a lot about them. There was one box that had a bug that wasn't even from this part of the country and I wondered how you would even get something like that.

Then Mrs. Ehrlman asked to see the insects. Aaron handed her a box.

"These are Longhorned Beetles," he said.

Mrs. Ehrlman raised the box and pulled the white lid off to look inside. I don't know what she was expecting to see, but I'm pretty sure it wasn't three adult Longhorned Beetles flying out of the box into her face.

I had no idea the insects were alive. And I guess Mrs. Ehrlman didn't either. I guess most people collect dead insects, not living ones.

She screamed so loud that the rest of the gym went quiet. She was swinging her arms and batting at the bugs with her hands. Mr. Monroe was trying to help but didn't seem like he wanted to hit Mrs. Ehrlman to try to get them.

Meanwhile, Aaron Decker was just standing there looking shocked. I had never seen him look so confused.

Then it was all over. Well, mostly over. Mrs. Ehrlman stopped screaming. Mr. Monroe was straightening his suit jacket. And three dead Longhorn Beetles were on the gym floor.

Aaron stared at the three lifeless insects, then took the white box that had dropped to the ground, and slid the dead bugs into it. He looked inside and I'm pretty sure I saw him look sad.

I was watching him when I realized Mrs. Ehrlman and Mr. Monroe were standing in front of me. They both still looked a bit rattled.

I didn't know how science teachers could be bothered by bugs, but guess they were.

"Mr. Noonan, is it?" Mr. Monroe said. "Would you care to explain and demonstrate your project?"

They seemed distracted, so I knew I had to do my best.

"Yes. I've built a seismometer, a device that measures the strength of an earthquake using the

Richter scale." I turned and lifted the box off the top of my project. I swear I saw Mrs. Ehrlman take a step back as I raised it.

I hadn't even looked at it since early in the day when I boxed it up. Since then, I'd seen all the other projects come into the gym, and for the first time I realized how good it was. The wooden upside down L structure was painted in bright red and secured into the plaster of Paris foundation in the litter box. The fishing line hung off the end of the bar with the plumb and pencil dangling—the pencil tip just barely touched the paper roll. The paper stretched out from the roll and was connected to the small electric motor holding an empty spool to take in the paper.

I stared at all of it and was proud of myself. I'd built this. Sure, I had help from Felix with the idea, and from Mr. Kaplan at the hardware store for picking out the pieces. But isn't that what scientists do? They get help. They talk. They test, and they build.

Mr. Monroe moved closer and inspected my build.

"This is really well constructed, Mr. Noonan," he said.

"Thanks." I'm pretty sure I was blushing.

I noticed a bunch of other kids come closer to watch and listen.

"Does it work?" Mrs. Ehrlman said.

"It doesn't exactly gauge the strength on the Richter scale, but it does work," I said.

I turned to it and hesitated. That had been the hardest part, getting the motor to turn and pull the paper roll at the right speed. Too slow and the pencil marks went on top of each other. Too fast and the paper spun off the roll to the floor. I had rolled that paper up the night before more times than I cared to remember.

I pushed the switch I'd taken from my electronic circuitry toy set from a couple Christmases ago, and the electric motor came on and started turning. Paper fed from the spool onto the wooden dowel connected to the motor.

Both Mrs. Ehrlman and Mr. Monroe let out little sounds of admiration. An "Ooh," from her and a "Well look at that," from him. Though they may have just been happy not be attacked by insects again.

I put my left hand on the table and started

tapping and shaking it just a little bit.

"This is to simulate the earthquake," I said. "An earthquake is the sudden slip of the tectonic plates along what is called a fault line."

The motor kept pulling paper and now the plumb was reacting to the movement of the table and began to swing back and forth, ever so slightly. The pencil left light marks on the paper as it passed underneath.

I shook harder. The plumb moved more and the pencil marks grew bigger. I lifted my hand off the table, and the plumb slowed and then stopped. After the line continued on for a few seconds with no movement, I pushed the switch to turn the motor off.

CHAPTER 17

I was confused and excited at the same time, if that were possible. But I couldn't stop staring at the trophy on the car seat beside me that seemed to tower over my head. The plastic was made to look like metal, but I didn't care. It was the first trophy I'd ever won.

My dad was smiling bigger than I was. He was driving Mom's station wagon and she had the twins in his car. I was glad to have that time alone, and with Dad, before getting home.

He drove right past our street and kept going. He saw me look behind us as Prosperity Lane flew by. I looked up at him in the rear view mirror.

"Figured we could do a little celebrating," he said. "Just you and me."

He stopped at the ice cream shop in the strip mall where the hardware store was. We never get real ice cream. Mom makes her own with like three ingredients in a big wood bucket. She says it's healthier that way. But it's ice cream. The point of ice cream isn't to be healthy.

I had a mint chocolate chip waffle cone and Dad had a fudge sundae. We both smiled the entire time. He kept asking me to tell him about what I said to the judges, what they said, and how it felt being called onto the small stage at the back of the gym to receive my trophy.

But I couldn't even remember. It was all a blur.

There were much better projects there. I mean, the windmill actually made electricity and stored it in a car battery. But Dad said he thinks I won because my project was good, and it looked like I built it myself.

Mom looked us up and down when we got home. She knew we'd gone somewhere, but didn't know where. She hugged me and looked at the trophy, then moved a photo of her and Dad when they got married from over the fireplace and put it right there for everyone to see. I didn't tell her I kinda wanted it in my room.

Dad kept asking the twins if they had anything to say to me.

Janis said, "Good job, Moon."

Ian said, "Good poopy poop, Mr. Poopy."

From him, that was a compliment.

I went to my room and closed the door. The quiet felt good after being in the crowded gym all day. I dialed the phone. On the fifth ring, Felix's mom answered.

"It's Mo. Can I talk to Felix?"

It was loud on the other end of the phone line and I could barely hear her.

"I'm sorry, Mo. Felix is really busy right now," she said. "He can call you later."

It was already 5:30 and Mom would have dinner ready soon.

"I really, really need to talk to him," I begged. "I have a lot of good news to tell him."

I hadn't even had the chance to tell him about

making the soccer team, then there was the surprising science fair win.

More noise. It sounded like a bunch of kids screaming, which made no sense since Felix is an only child.

"Okay," she said. "Let me see if I can get him for just a minute."

I strained to hear what was going on while the phone was sitting on the table waiting for Felix to come pick it up. Was that the sound of a stick hitting a piñata?

"Mo?" Felix said.

"Felix! I have so much to tell you," I said. "But, what's going on there? Are your parents having a party?"

"Well," he said, then he "umm'ed" a lot.

"Felix?"

"It was a surprise. I had no idea about it," he said.

"About what?"

"Mom got the other homeschooled kids and threw me a surprise birthday party," he said.

All of the excitement of the day drained out of me. All the stories I wanted to tell him were gone. Not just about winning the science fair, but about the beetles flying into Mrs. Ehrlman's face, the drone crashing, and of course about making the soccer team.

"But your birthday isn't for two more weeks," I said.

"I know! We'll do something on my birthday, I promise," Felix said. "I'll have another party or you can come for a sleepover."

I heard his mother asking him to come back to the party.

"I really gotta go, Mo," he said. "I'm sorry."

The phone clicked.

CHAPTER 18

Mom could tell something was wrong, but she didn't ask me about it. Which was strange because she was usually all "What's going on?" and "Are you feeling okay?" if you showed the slightest hint of not being happy.

Everything wasn't okay, but it should have been. I won the science fair for fifth grade and would compete for the Tall Pines Elementary trophy. After breakfast, Mom was taking me to buy my soccer uniform. I should have been the happiest kid on earth.

But all I could think about was Felix having

a birthday party without me. We've been best friends and at each other's parties since we were in preschool.

In kindergarten he lost a tooth and was so upset that I pulled one of my own out right there in front of him so we would match. It was already wiggly and going to come out on its own any second, but it made him happy. He stopped crying and we both got little orange plastic treasure chest boxes to put our teeth in. I never told Mom and Dad about pulling my own tooth, especially with Dad being an orthodontist.

Mom parked in front of Corner Kick Soccer. We sat in silence for a few minutes. I tried to make myself get happy. All the bright colored jerseys hanging in the store window in front of the car helped. Soon, I'd have my own.

"Okay. I'm ready," I said.

Sunday afternoon was when kids on my team were supposed to pick up their uniforms, so I hoped I would get to see some of the boys I'd be playing with.

We went in and there were several other kids in line to get their uniforms. One was Billy

Lanister from Ms. Gonzales' class, so at least I knew someone on my team, even if we weren't really friends. At least we weren't enemies.

Billy turned around with a jersey in his hands and a smile on his face. A big number one was on the back. I hadn't even thought of what number I'd be. Do I get to choose?

We stepped up to the counter when my name was called.

The man pulled a bag from a box.

"Noonan, Mo," he said.

"That's me."

"Looks like you are number four."

Four. I could handle that. Four was a good number. An even number. I liked four.

He opened the bag and pulled out the jersey. As soon as he held it up, I could tell it was huge. It was probably actually normal sized for a fifth grader, but as I've said, I am *not* normal sized for a fifth grader.

The man looked at me then back at the jersey, which already had the big four on the back. I felt that sinking feeling you get when things don't go right. I should be used to it when it has to do with being small, but I've been looking forward to soccer for so long. Now it looks like I'll be wearing a dress to play in.

"Is there anything you can do about the size?" Mom said.

The man hesitated, looked down at me again, then nodded.

"I think I can," he said. "Don't need the boy tripping over his own jersey. Can you come back in an hour?"

More families were coming in to get their uniforms and it was getting filled up. I recognized a couple other boys on the way out.

Mom was trying to make everything seem fine.

"See? He's making your jersey and we'll come right back and pick it up."

But all it did was remind me of my smallness, and how much bigger the rest of the team, and the teams we would play, were going to be.

We walked around and looked in the windows of the other shops in the small complex. There weren't any big name stores like at the mall. We passed a candle shop and a place that seemed to only sell kites. I wanted to go in, but didn't ask.

At the end of the row was the ice cream shop Dad had taken me to.

When we got back to the soccer store, the man had a smaller jersey all ready for me. Mom held it up to me and it looked perfect. While I was looking at it and taking in the greatness of its glowing white beauty, the man called the next person who was waiting.

"Decker. White team. Number ten."

CHAPTER 19

Three more days of school. After Wednesday, it would be summer break. But before then, there was still the final science fair assembly on Monday, the first soccer practice with Aaron Decker on my team Tuesday night, and I didn't have Felix to talk to anymore.

I admit the last one was because of me. I hadn't tried to call him again since Saturday. He knew how to call me too, you know.

Dad had breakfast ready Monday morning. Homemade fruit loops, he said. The tone of his voice sounded like he didn't think they would taste good, either. I poured almond milk on them, pinched my nose, and ate. You don't think fruit loops could be smelly. But these were.

The only thing that made some of Mom's cooking creations better was that at school I got to pick my own lunch. That had been a battle. Up through second grade, she was still sending me with a bagged lunch. After a month of coming home with it uneaten, she finally gave in and put money on my school account. From then on it was square pizza, dry burgers with stale fries, and a pasta bake that looked like it was from a hundred years ago, and I loved all of it.

I left Dad with the twins and walked to school. The calm of the sidewalks on my street turned to the excitement of the last week of school as I got closer to Tall Pines Elementary. The halls were full of talking and laughter. I ignored it all.

I don't even think running into Aaron Decker right then would have bothered me. He could shove me or punch me all he wanted. It wouldn't hurt near as much as not getting invited to Felix's birthday party.

But Aaron didn't appear in front of me. I heard

a few kids say "Good luck!" to me as I passed. Thanks. I guess they were rooting for me for the science fair.

Into my classroom and to my desk, third row back, third row over, and put my backpack on the floor and sat down. There was chuckling and giggling around me.

I looked up.

On the white board were three different colors of letters spelling out, "Mrs. Noonan."

Then I saw her sitting behind Mrs. Baxter's desk. She was smiling at me.

CHAPTER 20

Oh, come on. Three days left of school and I got Mom as a substitute. What kind of teacher takes a day off the last week? That just seemed like something you shouldn't do.

I have to admit, it wasn't too bad. She was actually a pretty good teacher. The jokes she made at home that I thought were corny actually made kids laugh. It was still embarrassing and frightening, don't get me wrong, but it wasn't near what I expected.

After first recess it was time for science, but she didn't pick up the teacher's science book.

Instead, she sat on the edge of the desk and looked at the class.

"I'm a bit biased, but I know who I'll be rooting for in the science fair final at assembly later," she said.

My project was sitting in the corner of the room where it had been since the fair on Saturday.

"Mo, would you like to present your winning project to the class?"

I slunk down in my seat. Nobody wanted to see that.

"Yeah, Mo," Becky said. "Can you show us?"

"Please?" Ravi said.

What was weird was that they didn't sound like they were joking or being sarcastic.

"Really?" I said.

Almost everyone was nodding and looking at me. "Okay."

I got the box and Mom cleared space on the table with the overhead projector. After I looked around the room, I felt a bit of the excitement from Saturday. The accomplishment. The pride.

Then I told them about the seismometer and earthquakes. I shook the table and there were "oohs" and "ahhs" when the plumb moved and the pencil marked the paper.

When it was over I almost bowed. I had to keep myself from doing it. I'd never bowed in my life so I had no idea where that urge came from, and I'm glad I didn't.

At lunch kids were asking me about the project. It was mostly repeating everything I said in class, but it felt good.

Then finally the assembly came. The entire school was sitting on the floor and the bleachers. On the small stage was a row of six tables with six kids and six science projects.

We were in order of grade, so only one kid was to my left, sixth grader Bao Cheng. He had a computer he built himself that was running a robotic arm, that he also built. I looked at my seismometer. I won the fifth grade science fair. I never expected to do that. So losing at the all grades event wasn't even a big deal.

The younger kids to my right had the range of the more usual projects. Potatoes that made electricity. A space station built from LEGO. A hover car made with balloons and an egg carton.

We presented one by one, starting with first

grade. Kindergartners don't do the science fair. When it got to me, I heard my class clap, though it may have been my mom getting them to clap.

A sixth grader from the school AV club was walking around on stage with a video camera. Our projects, and our faces, projected up on the huge screen over the stage. The first grader was caught picking his nose. Twice. This thrilled the audience into laughter and groans of disgust simultaneously.

One more time, I gave my presentation. One more time I explained about earthquakes and tectonic plates shifting. About the Richter scale and how my model of a seismometer worked. I

talked about some of the largest earthquakes in history, and how strong they were.

The Otaki, Japan earthquake in 1984 was a 6.1 magnitude on the Richter scale. At a 6.0, books and pictures fall off the walls of well built homes and buildings. Older structures may collapse.

Los Angeles in 1994 had a 6.7.

And the Indian Ocean earthquake in 2004 was a 9.1.

Finally the moment came. I hit the switch to turn on the electric motor.

There was a buzzing. The paper moved about half an inch, then stopped. I tasted the pasta bake from lunch come back up my throat a little.

Principal Juliano walked over to me to see what was wrong. My face must have been pretty white and looked like I was about to throw up.

"I…I…guess the batteries are dead," I was able to mutter. "I just showed it in class and it must have drained them."

The whole school was starting to talk and get restless. A few laughs grew and were followed by teachers saying "Shhh." Up until then I had them in my hands. They had all been listening to me.

I turned to step back to the side of my table. Defeat accepted. I still had my fifth grade win.

Then Bao Cheng came over from his table.

"What size do you need?" He said.

"What?" I was confused.

"What size batteries?" Bao said.

"Oh, uhh." I looked down at my seismometer and felt like I'd never even seen it before. "Umm…two double A."

Bao stepped back to his table, picked up the wireless mouse to his homemade computer, and popped two double A batteries out, then handed them to me. I stared at them in my hand, forgetting what to do with them for a moment, then replaced the old ones.

I tried to recover. I looked out at the audience, which had grown quiet again, then hit the switch.

The motor hummed the familiar tone and the paper roll started moving. The girl from AV Club moved in beside me and zoomed in on the plumb. I put my hand on the table and shook it gently. The plumb began its movement. The pencil marked the paper. And on the big screen above us, everyone saw it.

I shook the table a little harder. The plumb moved faster. Then I stopped, worried that the project would break or the table would fall apart. Once the pencil was making a straight line, I turned the electric motor off.

You may not believe this, because if you told me this had happened to someone, especially me, I would say you were lying, but everyone clapped. The whole gymnasium. Kindergarten through sixth grades. It was a blur of faces. I found my class, who looked the most excited. My mom was smiling. And to the left of them, Ms. Gonzales' class.

Aaron Decker wasn't clapping.

CHAPTER 21

The judges took a long time to vote. Way too long for having an entire elementary school waiting in the gym. The sixth grader always won. Why didn't they just get it over with?

Mrs. Juliano stepped up to the microphone. The girl with the video camera was beside her, broadcasting her up onto the screen. But Mrs. Juliano was a lot taller and the view on the screen was pointed up her nose.

"First, I need to congratulate all of our class winners for an incredible set of projects this year," she said. "This has truly been the best science fair I've had the privilege of overseeing."

We were lined up behind her, still standing with our tables. I looked at my seismometer. A collection of scrap wood, fishing line, and a kitty litter box. It was basic. It was simple. It shouldn't have been exciting. Bao Cheng made a robot arm write his name on a dry erase board, after I gave him his batteries back. I made a weight move back and forth and draw a pencil line.

"This is a first in Tall Pines Elementary history," Ms. Juliano said. "I'd like to announce the winner… Bao Cheng—"

The audience cheered but there were some boos as well.

"And Mo Noonan. For the first time we have a tie for first place!"

The whole gym erupted, even though no volcanoes were allowed in the science fair.

CHAPTER 22

Goodbye, fifth grade. It felt different, though. The last week of the year had been great. Some parts before that weren't so good. The whole getting bullied and punched parts. And of course not talking to Felix anymore. That was the worst part. But the science fair was awesome.

I had a promise to make good on, and Mom agreed to drive me. She pulled up in the loading zone of the hardware store. I took my project from the back of her car. Janis and Ian were screaming about one of them touching the other one.

"I'm just going to park and wait with the littles," she said. "Is that okay?"

You have no idea. "It's fine, Mom," I said.

The electric door slid open. Mr. Kaplan was just finishing with a customer.

"Mo Noonan!" he said. "I heard you did well with your project."

"I won, Mr. Kaplan. I won the fifth grade science fair then I tied for the all-school trophy," I said.

He looked as proud as Dad had been.

"Would you like to show me?" he said.

I set the box on the end of the tall counter and he helped lift the box off since it was so high.

"This looks amazing, Mo."

I blushed. "Thanks."

I didn't give him the full science fair speech, but I showed him the basics. He nodded and smiled. When the motor came on I thought he was going to clap.

Some customers came over to see. I got handshakes and pats on the back.

"Mo, would you be willing to let me display this in the window for a week or two?" he said.

I glanced over at the big window at the front of the store. Usually it was filled with gardening tools or rafts to go in your swimming pool.

"That would be pretty cool, Mr. Kaplan."

The folding display board was in the back of Mom's station wagon, so I ran to get that and told her what was happening. You'd have thought I had a painting getting hung in a museum in New York City the way she reacted.

By the time I got back into the hardware store, Mr. Kaplan had my seismometer on a table in the window. We set the board behind it just as it had been at the science fair.

Summer started pretty well.

CHAPTER 23

I wanted to walk to the soccer field for my first practice, but Dad insisted on driving me. I didn't argue too much after walking in my new cleats out to the car. They weren't the most comfortable things.

For years Felix and I kicked the ball into the goal in his backyard. I'd been on a soccer field before, sure, but not to actually, you know, play soccer with a team. The pee wee team years ago played on the old grass fields at the high school. The green turf was so bright and felt good to walk on. The cleats finally made sense.

The large goals for big kids and adults were at the ends of the long field. There were smaller goals not too different from Felix's set up from sideline to sideline. A smaller field for smaller people. I don't think they had my kind of small in mind.

I saw a boy with a white jersey like mine sitting on a bench a field over and walked toward him. When I got closer, I saw the number ten on the back. Great. Aaron Decker.

What my mom said weeks earlier came to mind again. *Be nice. Try to be his friend.* That didn't go too well at tryouts. All I could think about is how the blood would stain my new white jersey.

He was sitting with his elbows on his knees just staring at the ground. I was about to say something. I didn't know what. *Hi. What's up? A lovely night for soccer, isn't it?*

Before I did, he reached his left hand over and pulled his right shirt sleeve up and rubbed his arm and shoulder.

His skin was shades of purple and black. I'd never seen bruises like them. His cast was off, so maybe it was from that? I felt like I was seeing something I shouldn't, and turned to walk away.

My water bottle swung on the hook on my backpack and hit the metal bench. Aaron jumped a little and turned around. He yanked his shirt sleeve back down.

"What are you looking at, runt?"

"Sorry…I…was, uhhh…just gonna…" Instead of completing any sentence, I walked away.

When practice started, we all lined up and Coach Javier had us stretch and do some exercises. I thought we were going to play soccer.

"Fifteen pushups," Coach said. He's from a country called Portugal and has a little accent, but not so heavy you can't understand him. But he still uses wrong words sometimes.

We all dropped to our bellies and started pushing. One benefit of being tiny is I don't weigh much, so I can actually do things like pushups and pull-ups even though I'm not that strong. I was on my ninth pushup and heard Coach talking down the line.

"What is wrong?" Coach Javier said.

"I'm just…" It was Aaron. "My arm hurts."

I didn't expect this to be Army boot camp, but

I guess the coach knew what he was doing. He was older, like in his sixties, and someone said he'd been on a team with the famous Brazilian soccer player Pele when he was young.

"If you are want to be on my team, you do the same exercises as everyone does," Coach said.

"Coach," I said it before I thought about saying it.

He walked over to me.

"Yes, son?"

I'd finished my pushups and was on my knees.

"Aaron just got a cast off his arm like a week ago," I said. "I think he still hurts a bit. It was a pretty bad break."

Nobody had ever known what happened to Aaron Decker's arm.

Coach looked over at Aaron. "That is right? You broke your arm?"

"I did," Aaron said. "Yessir."

"How did your arm break?" Coach said.

Aaron's face was blank for a moment and his eyes moved to look at me.

"He had a bad bike wreck, Coach," I said.

What was I doing? Why was I helping Aaron Freakin' Decker?

"He was trying to jump over a trash dumpster behind the school," I said. "I was there. It was really bad. An ambulance came and everything. We told the ambulance people he'd just fallen off his bike. Didn't want us getting in trouble."

I saw the few boys from my school look at each other in confusion. There were no stories that went around about Aaron Decker jumping a trash dumpster.

"Is that right?" Coach said. "A daredevil you are? If you are want to be on my team, no more of that crap. You got it? If you get injured, it's gonna be on my soccer field, not riding your bicycle."

Everyone else was done with pushups and Coach moved on to have us run five laps around the field. I was on my fourth lap when Aaron passed me on his fifth. He slowed up beside me for a second.

"I guess I should say thanks," he said.

"It's fine," I said. My breathing was heavy from running. "I just—"

"Thanks, runt." He took off running faster and made the left turn to go behind the goal.

CHAPTER 24

My entire body felt broken. It hurt to move my legs. It hurt to move my arms. And sitting up was out of the question. What did that coach do to us?

I had time while I was paralyzed and staring up at the ceiling to consider quitting the team. It wasn't at all what I expected, but I had never been on a real soccer team before. Before last night, building a seismometer was the hardest thing I'd ever done. But that didn't make every part of my body hurt.

Then there was Aaron. I don't think I earned

any points trying to help him with the coach. I probably made it worse. Who knew what he would do to me after that.

Mom kept saying I would feel better if I got moving around. She said sitting still my muscles would just stay tight. It was hard to believe that, but because the twins were being more annoying than usual, I left on my bike.

I'd never tell her, but Mom was right. With each turn of the pedal, each street I rolled down, my body felt better. I still hurt, but not as much. I explored new roads I'd never ridden on. The boundaries I was allowed to travel to expanded with each year I got older.

The source of the pain still stuck with me. Soccer practice. The last time I played on a team it was pee wee soccer and Felix's dad was the coach. We would run some drills then split into two groups and half of us would get yellow pennies that hung to our knees to go over our shirts to show which team we were on. Well, mine went to the ground.

It was definitely summer and the afternoon got hot. I wished I'd brought a bottle of water and decided to head home. Looking around, I didn't recognize any of the houses and started to worry.

As I pedaled harder to get to the next corner, a black SUV sped past me. It was so close I felt the wind off the huge vehicle. The red brake lights illuminated as it turned into a driveway right in front of me and screeched to a stop. I was only a house away from it and pulled up behind a tree, thinking it stopped for me. I was scared.

The back door opened and Aaron climbed out. He was so tall it wasn't even a stretch for him. I heard yelling from inside the car. A deep, loud voice. Aaron slammed his door and walked around the back. The yelling started again when the driver's door opened. I could see the top of Aaron's dad's head over the tall SUV. Makes sense why Aaron is so tall at his age.

I couldn't hear what his dad was saying, even though it was so loud. It just sounded like words booming out and frightened me. I rolled forward on my bike a little since the car was blocking my view, and watched as Aaron walked in the front door of his house. His dad was behind him, still yelling, and pushed Aaron from behind with both of his hands. The last thing I saw was Aaron falling forward into the darkness of the house.

My heart was thumping in my chest. I turned the bike around and pedaled fast, thinking about how Aaron had pushed me into the front door of Tall Pines Elementary. Two blocks later I saw the sign for Prosperity Lane and turned left. It was still another mile until I had my bike in the garage and was up in my room really wishing I could talk to Felix. The image of Aaron's father shoving him couldn't leave my head.

My dad grounded me from playing video games once because I yelled at him when I was mad at him for making me help with the yard work. He didn't yell back, he didn't push me.

What I was thinking couldn't be true. Could it?

Was my bully's father bullying him?

CHAPTER 25

I'd fallen asleep reading *The Phantom Tollbooth* in bed and woke up in the back seat of Dad's SUV with a twin on either side of me fighting over a cheese stick. It was still dark outside.

"What are we doing?" I said. "And how did I get in the car?"

"Mom decided last night that we needed a little break this weekend." From the sound of Dad's voice, he didn't really agree with her.

I had a blanket over me and lifted it up.

"But I'm still in my pajamas!" I said.

"Sorry I didn't dress you in your sleep," Dad

said. "Was hard enough carrying you to the car."

It was another two hours before we got to the rental house a block away from the beach. The sun was just coming up.

We'd stayed there before and Mom said she saw they had one night available and decided to take it. Dad said he wasn't sure it was worth a four hour drive each way for one night at the beach.

Mom had thrown together a couple small bags of clothes in the car, just enough for the night. Swimsuits and an extra change of clothes. Two changes of clothes for the twins since they were extra messy.

For not having known about the trip when I went to bed, I got very excited when we finally arrived at the small house. It was torture being so close without getting wet in the ocean. Standing outside the front door I swore I could hear the waves. The twins were in their bathing suits and screaming to get in the water, even though I knew they would both get scared and barely get their feet wet once we were there.

Once everyone was ready to go, we made the five-minute walk. The wait at the stoplight to cross the main road took longer than the entire trip. Dad was way behind us carrying the tote bag with towels and sunblock in it, two beach chairs for him and Mom, the beach umbrella that sits in our garage fifty-one weeks of the year, and a book that he thought he would be able to read while we played. That last part never worked out for him.

The beach was packed. Striped umbrellas were everywhere. Kids screamed in delight and horror, depending on how they felt about the big waves that made it difficult to actually play in the water.

I got bored after splashing in the surf for a while, having no one to play with. I saw groups of kids farther up and down the beach kicking a soccer ball at the edge of the water.

"Can I go for a walk?" I said.

Mom was busy trying to force the twins into having fun. Dad was sitting in the chair under the umbrella pretending to read, but he was actually watching Mom deal with the littles. I really don't think my dad likes the beach much.

"What?" Mom said.

I was afraid the longer it took for me to ask, the greater the chance she'd try to make me take one or both of the twins with me.

"Is it okay if I go for a walk," I said. "Maybe play with some of the other kids." I pointed toward the group close to my age.

"Sure. I guess. Just be careful." She looked around. "Be sure to know where we are so you can find us again. And don't go to the boardwalk."

I saw the lifeguard stand to my left and the entrance to the beach that was marked with a sign that said 21ST STREET.

"I got it, Mom."

Freedom. No littles. No Mom and Dad. I walked right at the water's edge, occasionally jumping left when a bigger wave sent water up higher onto the sand. The families that had set up closest to the water would all scramble to move everything they own, but there was nowhere for them to move to because there were so many people.

It was only one night away, but it felt like a week. For those hours I was able to not think about soccer practice or Aaron Decker. I thought about how I could be anyone I wanted, as long as my family wasn't nearby. I was getting close to the kids my age playing soccer and thought how I could make up a new name, pick a new town, and say anything I want. I could be an all new person for an hour or two.

Picking a new name was fun. Max was the first thing I came up with, but then thought of my height and skinny arms, and kept thinking. Luke. Yeah, Luke. Felix would get a kick out of that when I told him.

I walked toward the group of boys. I decided that Luke was more outgoing than me and would walk up and introduce himself. Moon wouldn't do that.

"Hey guys, I'm Lu—"

"Mo?" A girl's voice behind me.

CHAPTER 26

I jumped a little and turned. Debbie Schultz was getting up from a towel on the sand.

"Mo Noonan, what are you doing here?" she said.

I didn't even think she knew my first name, much less my last name. So much for Luke.

"My family just came for the weekend," I said. "I didn't even know we were coming until this morning."

"I'm glad you did," she said.

She's glad I did?

"Where are you staying?" She said.

I barely heard her.

"Oh, we have a house a couple minutes from the beach," I said. "What about you?"

"My stepdad has a condo over there," she said. "He rents it out most of the time, but my mom makes him let us use it at least one week every summer. She always says we should come more, but he says it's an investment."

She turned and pointed to one of the tall buildings that offered every condo a view of the beach and ocean.

"That's cool," I said. That's cool. *That's cool?* Real smooth, Mo.

"Where are you headed to?" she said.

"I was just taking a walk. My brother and sister were driving me crazy."

"Can I come with you?"

"What? Oh, sure, of course," I stuttered.

She told her mom she was going, pulled a pair of shorts on over her swimsuit, and next thing I knew I was walking on the beach with Debbie Schultz. I can't tell you what we talked about, because I don't remember. It was a blur. She laughed at one point, put her hand on my shoulder, and said, "You are so funny, Mo. Why didn't I know you're so funny?"

I shrugged. That was my response.

Kids ran in front of us kicking balls and splashing water as parents yelled from their lounge chairs under brightly colored umbrellas. A boy screamed as his dad tried to get him to jump into one of the waves, which was taller than the dad. I love the beach, but never really enjoyed getting in the water here. The waves scare me a bit. Don't think I'll tell Debbie that. I just hope she doesn't suggest jumping into one.

The long pier stuck out into the water ahead of us and the beach was even more packed with people and umbrellas. The grey wooden buildings of the boardwalk were to our right now. People in swimsuits walked and rode bicycles past all of the shops selling airbrushed T-shirts, french fries, ice cream, and anything else you could imagine.

"Let's go to the boardwalk!" Debbie pulled some money from the pocket in her shorts. "I'll get us some saltwater taffy."

I must have stopped walking right where I was. Debbie had gone a few more steps then turned to look at me.

"You okay?" she said.

I wasn't. Debbie Schultz just asked me to go to the boardwalk and I can't. I mean, I could, but I'd be going against the one thing my mom told me not to do. Luke would have gone to the boardwalk. But I'm not Luke.

"I…I can't," I said. It hurt so badly to say. "My mom said not to go to the boardwalk."

I tried not to visibly cringe in preparation of being laughed at. But the laughter didn't come. Instead, she smiled, and walked back toward me.

"That's fine. It's kinda smelly there during the day anyway," she said.

We walked without talking for a little bit, then I felt her hand brush against mine as our arms swung. My stomach turned into a huge, heavy stone. On the next swing, another brush, then from somewhere, I have no idea where, maybe it was the new me, Luke, coming out, on the next swing I took hold of her hand.

Any moment she would pull away from me, yell at me, ask what I thought I was doing, then run off ahead. In school she would never talk to me again and all the other kids would point and laugh at me when I walked past them. Mo Noonan tried to hold hands with Debbie Schultz. It would be the biggest news of sixth grade, ruining my final year at Tall Pines Elementary. Ruining my life.

But that didn't happen. She just held my hand. She held my hand and we kept walking.

I couldn't talk. I couldn't breathe. I became overly concerned about burping and farting and sneezing and anything else that might happen to cause her to pull her hand away from me. I thought about it so much I thought I was going to make it happen.

We talked more, I think. It was strange to talk about normal things while I was holding Debbie Schultz's hand, but I figured that was the normal thing to do. It wasn't like you would talk about holding hands.

In fifth grade there were only two couples. It's not like high school where you see it everywhere, probably. Veronica Ainsley and Ronny Jacobson were going out, whatever that means. Which was funny because Veronica liked to be called Ronnie, so they were Ronny and Ronnie. They really just hung out with each other all the time. I heard their families do a lot of stuff together like take vacations and have holiday parties.

Debbie stopped and I stopped beside her, her hand still in mine.

"My stepdad is taking me to play mini-golf tonight while Mom is playing cards with some friends," she said.

"Nice. That sounds like a lot of fun," I said.

"It can be, but he usually just sits by the exit while I play alone. Do you think your parents would let you come with me?"

I looked up the beach toward where my family was, though they were too far away to see.

"Yeah," I said. "I think so."

She smiled and turned. Her parents were sitting on towels right there beside us while we were holding hands. I was mortified but noticed Debbie didn't care if they saw us. Her stepdad was reading a small newspaper about houses and condos for sale and her mom was lying with her arms to her side to get as much sun as possible. It looked to me like she'd had enough already.

"Mom, can Mo come play mini-golf with me

tonight?" Debbie said.

Debbie's mom lowered her sunglasses and looked at us, a big smile across her face.

"Of course, sweetie," she said. "Invite his whole family if you like."

No. Do not do that. Please do not do that.

Debbie looked at me. "How about just you?"

I smiled. "I'd like that."

CHAPTER 27

Even in summer it can get chilly at the beach after the sun goes down. I had a pullover hoodie on with shorts and it was barely enough. Mom only packed for one night and didn't think I'd need jeans. I woke up in the car this morning in my pajamas and only had one pair of shorts, one T-shirt, my hoodie, and swim shorts in the small bag she packed for me and the littles. She even forgot to put any underwear in.

The mini-golf course was ocean themed, which wasn't surprising since you could smell the salt water it was so close to the beach. Each hole had its own decoration. The first hole was surrounded by fake sand and a beach umbrella covered most of the green area. The third hole had obstacles that looked like oversized kid's beach toys, like a bucket and a big red shovel. The actual hole was inside a sand castle. Everything was a little worn out and faded, but we were the only people there, at least. The mini-golf place we passed on the way had a real airplane on the roof of the building where you pay and there was a line down the sidewalk to get in.

Debbie took her third putt on the eighth hole. It bounced off the far wall and rolled back, barely missing. The fake grass was blue and a huge plastic great white shark looked like it was jumping out of it.

"That was so close!" she said.

"You were robbed," I said.

I took my putt and pulled up short on purpose. I didn't want to beat her.

"So you're playing soccer?" she said.

"Yeah. I'm not on the highest team, but it's fun." It made me think of Aaron Decker for the first time that day.

"When do you play a game?"

"Next Saturday," I said. "Guess that's why we went out of town this weekend."

On the ninth hole she sunk the ball on her second hit and picked it up out of the hole.

"Can I come?" she said.

"Come where?" I said.

"Your soccer game." She laughed and did the hand on my shoulder thing again. I liked that. "We go home Friday because someone has the condo rented starting Saturday."

"Sure. That would be cool," I said.

That's no pressure at all.

Her stepdad brought us to the mini-golf course but he sat on a bench over at the entrance staring at the same newspaper he had at the beach, just like she said he'd do. I saw him look up to see where we were a couple times. My dad would have been right there at every hole with us making corny jokes and asking Debbie who her orthodontist was.

"I had fun walking with you today," I said.

I saw her smile real big.

"Me too," she said. "You know, I'd never held anyone's hand before."

"Me either," I said.

"All year I liked when we lined up next to each other in the hallway," she said.

I thought about day after day walking next to her, trying to think of the right thing to say. She always seemed uninterested or bored.

"Really?" I said.

"Really," she said. "I was always too nervous to say anything."

She swung the putter gently. The ball came off of the metal head, bounced off two walls, then dropped into the hole.

"You got a hole in one!" I said.

"I've never gotten a hole in one!" She jumped up and down, then hugged me. I was very glad in that moment that Mom had made me take a shower before going out. I didn't need Debbie smelling the fishy ocean water on me.

After finishing the course, her stepdad picked her mom up at their condo building and we went to dinner near the pier. It was a nice place right over the ocean. I felt splashes of water a couple of times we were that close. It was seafood, which isn't my favorite, but I ate it like I had it all the time.

Her mom asked me a few questions about school and soccer. Other than that, they didn't bother us. Her stepdad was telling her mom about a condo he saw for sale.

Out of the restaurant, her stepdad gave her

some money and said to have fun and be careful.

"Mo," he said. "I asked your dad if you could go to the boardwalk with us and he said it was fine." I realized it was the first time he had spoken directly to me.

"He did?" I said. My dad doesn't have anything against the boardwalk, I was just never allowed there alone, or at night even if he was with me.

"He did. We won't be far behind you, though."

Debbie and I were only a few steps away from them when I felt her hand fall into mine again.

"Saltwater taffy?" she said.

"Definitely."

CHAPTER 28

I didn't want to go home, but Dad had work the next day. Debbie was going to be at the beach until Friday, which was five more days I could have taken walks with her. It was the longest car ride ever, between the twins fighting and Mom constantly asking me questions about my "date" the night before. I think I broke the world record for eye rolls on that drive.

When I wasn't thinking about Debbie, my thoughts went to Aaron. I kept wondering if I should tell Mom what I saw at his house, but it felt like I was butting into someone else's life.

The last person you'd want to snitch on is the guy who regularly shoves you to the ground and bloodies your nose. He already went to the principal's office because of her once, so it was really a miracle I wasn't dead already. But even though he seemed to like hurting me, I didn't think it was right if his dad was hurting him.

When Dad finally came to a stop in our driveway, I grabbed my bag from the back of the SUV, went in the house, up to my room, and closed the door.

The reality of being home set in. Soccer practice. Aaron Decker. All of it.

It was still early in the summer, so at least I have that. No school for another two and a half months.

The twins were screaming and Mom used her soft and gentle hippie voice on them to try to calm things down. They were mad because they finally wanted to get in the ocean now that we were four hours away from it. Mom tried all day Saturday and again Sunday morning to get them in the water but neither of them would get close.

I saw Debbie at the beach for a while Sunday

morning before we'd left. We took another long walk. She told me about her fish tank and her favorite angelfish that died a few weeks ago. Right as I was about to leave, she gave me a piece of paper. There was a drawing of a boy and a girl holding hands on it and her phone number.

"That's my cellphone. Mommy got me one a few months ago so I wouldn't always be using the phone at home while she was trying to talk to clients."

For some reason I was confused and just stared at the drawing and the number.

"So, will you call me?" she said. "I'm here the rest of the week and I'm going to be super bored without you here."

"Yeah," I'd said. "Of course I will."

There was a moment I thought about telling her about Aaron. About being bullied, and about what I had seen. The bruises. Him getting pushed at home. But I didn't. I decided that wasn't my story to tell. That was Aaron's story.

CHAPTER 29

Soccer practice began with the same exercises as the last time. I made sure I was at the other end of the line of boys from Aaron, and told myself a million times I wouldn't try to help him again.

My mom said to try to be his friend, or at least be friendly. I've done that. Even knowing what I thought I knew, it didn't make me want to be any closer to him.

There was no "runt" muttered as he ran past me on our laps. I took that as a small victory. I couldn't see any more bruises and he didn't have a cast on. But I couldn't stop thinking about what I saw from outside his house.

Coach Javier watched me during a drill where we ran through a line of cones, dribbling the ball in front of us, then took a shot on goal. He stopped me and had me do it again, out of order from the line of boys. I couldn't tell if I was doing something wrong or doing something right.

A few minutes later he pulled me aside.

"You're much better at shooting than I thought you would be," Coach Javier said.

"Thanks?" I wasn't sure if it was a compliment.

"But you are too small," he said.

There it is. Too small for soccer. It wasn't like I tried out for basketball.

"I can't do anything about that, Coach," I said, not knowing how to respond and feeling annoyed that a grown up, my own coach, would bully me about my height.

"No, no, no," he said. "Tall or short, it doesn't matter in soccer. It is the beautiful game. Have you heard that before? People call soccer the beautiful game."

I hadn't.

"You just learn to play different. You have to play better, be faster, be smarter," he said.

It all made sense, but I didn't know where he was going with it.

"Soccer is a team. You have ten other players on the field. We just have to find what works."

Coach looked over to the line of boys still practicing with the assistant coach, then yelled.

"Send that one over, the big one," he said.

The big one? You mean Aaron Decker?

Aaron started walking over.

"Run," Coach yelled.

He sped up a little. Finally he was beside me.

Coach looked at us, back and forth. His eyes went up to Aaron, and down to me, up to Aaron, and down to me.

"Yes, yes," he said.

We spent the next half hour working on drills together. Coach kept having us try different things, switching positions and formations as we practiced getting the ball down field and into the goal.

There was a glimpse of something with Aaron I hadn't seen before. He seemed to be enjoying it. I even saw him practice some footwork while we were on a water break. At one point I swear I saw him smile.

Dad let me walk to soccer practice, but said he'd be over to the field to watch and pick me up. It was a compromise I had taken because I really don't like walking home alone after dark. He was sitting over on a bench watching us practice and making notes in his little book.

"What were the two of you doing over there?" he said.

I looked back at the field and saw Aaron walking down the sidewalk carrying his water bottle.

"Coach just had us running some drills."

CHAPTER 30

I was nervous. There's no way I could say I wasn't. The breakfast Mom made sat in front of me uneaten. It was homemade bagels that were round, with no hole, as hard as a golf ball, and scrambled eggs made with coconut milk. So that probably wasn't getting eaten anyway.

Dad didn't even argue to drive me to the field. I think he could tell I needed the walk. It was time out of the house, alone, between the craziness of the twins and my very first real soccer game.

I was halfway there, not paying attention to anything, when a big car stopped beside me. The back door flew open and Debbie jumped out.

"I'll see you there, Mom," she said, then slammed the door.

"You're actually coming to the game?" I said.

"Of course I am."

There were moments I thought I had imagined the walks on the beach and the mini-golf with Debbie, even though we talked on the phone almost every day since then. But she was really here beside me again, and she took my hand as we walked down Prosperity Lane toward the soccer fields.

"You nervous?" she said.

"Nah," I said. "It's just a game."

I saw her grin. She knew.

I saw a couple boys from my team on the far side when we got to the field.

"Well, I'd better get over there," I said.

"Good luck, Mo." She leaned in and gave me a tight hug. "You're going to do great."

"Thanks."

"See you after?" she said.

"Sure."

I jogged across the field to my team. One of

the boys from my school looked at me, then over to the stands. "Was that Debbie Schultz?"

"Yup," is all I said.

The ref motioned to the coaches and we took the field. The other team looked huge, like they-drove-themselves-to-the-game huge. They wore red jerseys, red shorts, and red socks. I didn't recognize any of them since they were from twenty miles away. They were the Eagles. I didn't know there were red eagles. Hawks, maybe.

I was playing midfield. Aaron was to my right. He hadn't said a word to me during warmups. Jeremy Robinson and Sung-hoon Lee were at forward.

The whistle blew. Jeremy tapped the ball to Sung-hoon and we were playing soccer. I always thought that it would feel different. That once it was a real game, everything changed. But it wasn't too different than our scrimmages, except we didn't know the boys in the bright red uniforms.

They played rough, but we had Aaron and a couple other big kids. There were a few penalties on both sides resulting in free kicks. The Eagles scored first. A few minutes later Sung-hoon kicked a perfect cross from the left and Jeremy punched it right in. Their goalie flew through the air to try to get it, but missed by a mile.

The whistle blew and both teams went to their benches for halftime. I collapsed on the ground with my water raised over my head and drank half of it. After sitting up, I looked across the field to the stands. Debbie saw me looking and waved. Then I saw another hand waving. It was Felix. His mom was beside him on the first row of the small bleachers. I waved back and both Debbie and Felix thought that I was waving at them, which I guess I was.

Halftime was over so quick. I was substituted for a few minutes and was kneeling on the ground. Aaron was ten feet from me. Coach Javier came over to us.

"Are you two ready?" he said.

I looked at Aaron, who gave no reaction, then nodded to Coach.

"Yessir," I said.

I turned back to Aaron. "Right, Aaron?"

He nodded. "We're ready."

The next time the ball was kicked out, we got put back in the game. We were both in midfield again. I kept watching for the opportunity, but the ball was never in the right place. I got a foot on it once, but it was taken away and I was knocked flat on the ground. I watched the play go on without me, then got up and brushed the black rubber turf off my knees.

It was 2-to-2 and Coach was yelling time was almost up. Jeremy was out of the game saying his ankle hurt, and Sung-hoon was looking winded.

An Eagle threw the ball in from the side. It bounced off one of their own player's feet and was taken by Brandon Wheeler on our team. He dribbled forward to just before midfield. Aaron went running across in front of him just as Brandon released the ball and Aaron took it.

By then I was behind Aaron. Nobody was covering me. There were three bright red Eagles all over Aaron, but they were already scared of him and not getting too close. He had better ball control than I thought he would, for such a big kid.

He sent the ball a little too far ahead and an Eagle crossed over to steal, but Aaron lunged forward. His right foot went between the other player's legs and tapped it just out of reach. The kid went rolling on the ground in a mess of shiny red material and dirt.

It was happening. It was working.

Closer to goal and I was still behind Aaron as he dribbled the ball down the field. More red players came from either side. They looked so huge and like there were more of them than us. Some white jerseys from our team were moving to block them.

Right down the middle of the field. It probably lasted less than ten seconds in total, but felt like ten minutes.

The keeper came forward out of goal as we got closer to cut the angle. Aaron tapped the ball and moved left. So many red players were coming at us. I stayed right behind Aaron until we were almost to the keeper, then I cut to my right and ran as fast as I could.

And just like Coach said, nobody followed me. *They never cover the small guys*, he said.

I looked left just as Aaron was releasing the ball, but instead of kicking toward the goal, he tapped a strong pass to the right. The keeper was out of position and every Eagle was flying toward Aaron. I was wide open with an empty goal in front of me.

The inside of my foot connected with the ball. It changed direction and went a few feet in the air and farther right than I wanted, toward the right post of the goal, but then it dropped, hit the ground, and spun left into the goal.

CHAPTER 31

It was a blur of high-fives and congratulations. I wasn't sure who was even around me.

"Couldn't have done it without Aaron," I said so many times, to each person who slapped me on the back and said, "Great goal."

I found Aaron, already off by himself. He pretended to not see me walk up to him.

"Great job, Aaron," I said.

He shrugged. "Whatever. Wasn't hard."

"Okay, well, good game," I said. "We make a good team."

He took his water bottle and backpack and

headed off across the field. There was no black SUV waiting for him.

Felix came running onto the field and I was waving at him. He stopped a few feet from me when we both seemed to realize we hadn't talked in what seemed a lifetime.

"Hey, Mo."

"Hey, Felix."

"Sorry I haven't called you back," he said.

"It's okay."

Like that we were best friends again, though I don't think we ever weren't. We had a lot to catch up on.

Debbie ran up and gave me a big hug. Felix looked like he was going to fall over.

"Do you remember Felix?" I said. "He was in our class in first grade."

"Of course I do," she said. Then she gave him a big hug, too.

Debbie turned back to me. "I asked your parents if you could go for ice cream with us and they said yes," she said.

"Really?"

"Yes, silly."

"Okay," I said. "I'll be right there."

Debbie ran off across the field to her parents. Felix was staring at me.

"Do…do you have a girlfriend?" he said.

"I don't really know. I wasn't trying to get one, but guess it kinda happened."

Felix's mom called for him. He waved at her.

"Well, guess I'd better go." Felix said. "Want to come over and play soccer tomorrow?"

"Sure."

"Oh, and I guess I'll see you tonight, too," he said.

"Tonight? What's tonight?"

"The singing thing at the coffee shop," he said.

"The what?"

"Your dad's thing."

"What are you talking about?"

"The open mic thing." His mom called for him again. "I better go. See you tonight!"

CHAPTER 32

I felt like my brain had exploded. Dad was doing an open mic night.

He was singing and playing guitar.

In public.

In front of real people.

And he invited my best friend's family.

I don't even remember eating ice cream with Debbie. Only the mint chocolate chip colored stain on my white soccer jersey proved it actually happened. All I could think about was my dad standing on stage.

I threw myself on the mercy of the court

and asked to stay home. They would have to understand. Wouldn't they? They were kids once. I think.

But they didn't understand.

"This is a special night for your father," Mom said. "Can't you let him have this? He's been working so hard on the songs."

"Songs? Plural? As in more than one song?" I said.

"Oh, sweetie," she said. "The world isn't only about you."

Turns out they had invited Debbie and her parents, too. So the embarrassment was even bigger.

I had a good run, at least. Does witness protection help embarrassed fifth graders?

I'd been in the coffee shop with Dad a hundred times. Maybe a thousand. He always ordered the same thing: a double shot of espresso. I know he doesn't like the organic coffee Mom buys for the house, so he stops there whenever he can. He never said not to tell Mom he gets their coffee, but I just knew not to.

Walking into the shop tonight it felt huge. It

was darker in the back part of the room than usual and rows of tables were set up with forty-eight chairs. Plus all the regular seats in the coffee shop and places to stand. And it was already filling up.

The small stage had two large speakers and a microphone stand. A row of lights I had never noticed hung from the ceiling and lit everything on the small stage.

"Dad." I tugged on his sleeve. "There's a lot of people here. You sure you want to do this?"

He looked around, then rubbed my hair with his hand. "No, I'm not buddy. But I gotta try. You'll understand one day. Sometimes there's things you just feel like you gotta do, no matter how much they scare you."

I did understand. I'd done one of them that morning out on the soccer field. I'd also walked up to Aaron and talked to him several times like Mom had asked. Both of those things scared me, but I did them.

There were three tables up front with little cardboard tents that said RESERVED. One was for Felix's and Debbie's families. The other was for

Dad's partners from his orthodontist practice. I couldn't believe he *wanted* people he knew to see this.

Once the show started, there were three people before him. Two were singers like him, except they could actually sing, and the other read a long poem about a horse and a soldier in a war that seemed like it took place in the future. It really lost me.

Then it happened. My dad was called onto the tiny stage, which all of a sudden looked huge. He walked up to the mic stand and plugged a cable into his guitar. It let out a huge popping sound.

"Sorry," he said. "First time."

He looked nervous but I think I was shaking even more than he was. He picked at each string and adjusted the tuning. Then he did possibly the worst thing he could do. He talked.

"Hi there," he said. There was a loud squeak of feedback before the teenager at the soundboard adjusted for it. "I'm Dan Noonan. Some of you may know me from putting braces on your children's teeth."

Oh, no. Orthodontist jokes.

"But tonight I'm going to do something different. And don't worry, I'm not quitting my day job."

I could tell he had worked himself up to the moment. He probably thought he could say a few things then just start singing and playing, but that didn't happen.

He froze.

For like almost a minute.

The fingers on his left hand were stretched into the shape of a chord on his Martin guitar. His right hand held the pick an inch away from the strings. The whole room sat silent and still with him. A few people in back gave soft claps of encouragement.

Everybody heard him take a deep breath in, then the air blew right into the mic, causing another loud sound.

"You can do it, Dad," I said. In the silence it was loud. I hadn't even meant to say it. It just came out. Even in my embarrassment I urged him on. I'd heard him play a billion times at home, and sing old songs in the living room while the twins stared up at him like an arena audience.

He looked over at me and I saw him smile, and he looked relaxed.

Then he started to play the guitar. My whole body tightened. I don't think I was breathing and am pretty sure my heart stopped beating, even though I know that's impossible.

I didn't recognize the song. He used to play around the house all the time but right then I realized I hadn't heard him in a while.

Debbie was on my left and Felix on the other side. Right before Dad was about to start singing, Debbie took my hand and held it as they hung between our chairs. I felt myself breathe again.

When my dad started singing, his voice was familiar, but the song wasn't. I stopped listening just to the sound of his voice and paid attention to the words.

I really thought it was going to sound like the old hippie music he and Mom listened to all the time, but it didn't. It sounded like something new.

And it was good.

The tension in my shoulders went away. I saw

Felix tapping his hand to the beat. Debbie's fingers tightened on mine.

After the first song, Dad stopped for a moment. People actually clapped for him. I did, too.

"I appreciate you humoring me tonight in my debut and swan song," he said. "I always dreamed of singing on a stage one day, but never thought I really would. To me, this coffee house is as good as Carnegie Hall."

More quiet applause.

Dad always made jokes about Carnegie Hall whenever he played guitar around the house. He said it's an old theater in New York City where only the most famous people get to perform.

"I have one more song for you. I wrote this one over the last few weeks about someone very special to me," he said.

Oh, no. A sappy love song about Mom. Is there a shell I can crawl into?

"My life wouldn't be the same," he said. "This is called 'Over the Moon'."

What?

I'd heard the opening notes of the song a couple of weeks ago when I came in from Felix's house, then he'd stopped playing when he heard me. I didn't think anything of it then.

He glanced over at me and smiled as he played the beginning of the song, then looked out over the audience with his mouth to the microphone.

My light, my reason
My being, my son
Without you I would be no one

You came to us
In a deep winter freeze
And warmed our hearts
And you brought out the sun

I was over the moon from the first moment I saw you
I was over the moon the first time you cried
I was over the moon whenever I held you
You are my sun and my moon.

CHAPTER 33

Dad smiled all day Sunday, even while mowing the lawn and washing the cars. He kept saying he had a lot of extra energy and wouldn't stop finding new things to do. The box of projects in the garage was actually emptied a little.

I was proud of him. And not just because he didn't embarrass me that badly. But because he did something he always wanted to do.

After the celebrations were over, life went back to normal like nothing happened. My soccer win was a memory with the next practice coming up fast, then another game, and another after that.

I spent most of Sunday with Felix, but Monday he was on a field trip with his homeschool friends, even though it was summer break, which sounds like a nightmare. So I packed a lunch and went out for the day on my own. Better than being stuck at home with the twins screaming.

There was only so far I could ride my bike, even with the newly expanded borders Mom set, but I took full advantage of every street, every corner. I sat at a park I'd never been to and ate my sandwich and drank my juicebox.

I couldn't imagine a better day.

As I got back on my bike, a large black SUV sped past me. The tires squealed as it turned a corner. I recognized it. It was Aaron's dad's car. I thought about riding behind it and stopping to talk to him, to see if he wanted to play a game or kick a soccer ball. But I didn't. Some things are just too scary.

My dad had written a song about me, then sang it in front of a lot of people, even though he was scared. Mom makes weird food that I can honestly say scares me sometimes, but I know she's just trying new things and wants us to be healthy. She's always pushing Dad to lose five pounds, though he doesn't look like he needs to. And she keeps saying she needs to lose ten, which I don't understand either.

I was so scared and embarrassed thinking about my dad singing in public, and afterward I probably clapped harder than anyone. Hard not to when the song is about you. The twins even sat still and listened the whole time he was on stage. I think that was a record for them.

I did ride down Aaron's street, but didn't stop. The SUV was there and the front door was closed. I didn't hear anything. No yelling. But I thought about what I'd seen the first time I'd gone down that road and how Aaron looked falling into the house after his father pushed him.

My dad never spanked me or shoved me like I saw Aaron's dad do to him.

I saw those bruises on Aaron's arm and shoulder at practice, and the broken arm at school a while back and never thought anything about it back then.

Dad always wanted to come to my soccer practice. Aaron walked alone or got dropped off.

I barely saw his dad that one time and have never seen his mom. Some kids say she used to be a teacher in their old town, but isn't anymore.

It's easy as a kid to think the world is against you just because you can't get a video game you want or your little brother and sister keep going in your room to play with your stuff. But some kids have a lot more to worry about.

I was riding back down Prosperity Lane to go home when I let all the little things I'd been thinking about come back together into one big thought. That Aaron's father is hurting him. The moment I did, I felt my body go cold, even though it was probably ninety degrees outside and I was sweating from riding my bike all day.

But I swear, my whole body shivered. I realized some things shouldn't be kept a secret, no matter how afraid you are.

A block from home I stopped pedaling and got off my bike, unable to move for a few minutes. I sat down on the curb to think some more about what I would say and how it would sound out loud. I had felt it wasn't my story to tell, and never had. Not to Felix. Not to Debbie. Before I realized it, I was crying. I didn't even care if someone I knew drove by and saw me. I just sat there crying.

I hoped I was wrong and everything I thought was a mistake, things seen differently than they really are. An optical illusion. Kids have bike wrecks and break their arms and bruise their shoulders. Maybe he tripped walking into the house and his dad was trying to catch him.

But I knew I wasn't wrong.

I thought again about Dad saying that sometimes there's things you just feel like you gotta do, no matter how much they scare you. And this scared me. I knew I had to do something, but I wasn't sure what. I was only a kid.

But Aaron is only a kid, too, even though he's the biggest kid I've ever seen. And even though he hits me and calls me runt, no matter what he does to other people, his dad shouldn't hurt him. No grown up should hurt a kid, especially their own son.

I made up my mind and got back on my bike to get home and talk to Mom.

CHAPTER 34

I dropped my bike on the front yard, just like I'm not supposed to, and ran into the house. I could barely breathe from riding so hard, but I had to find her and talk to her before I changed my mind.

The twins were upstairs fighting over something, but Mom wasn't with them trying to sort it out all quiet and peaceful like.

I found her in the kitchen.

She was sitting at the table alone. Her hands were on either side of a full glass of water.

And she looked sad.

I'd never seen her like that before. It made me stop right where I was and just stare at her for a minute before I could say anything.

"Mom? Are you okay?"

She reached her hand out and put it on the table in front of the chair next to her.

"Sit down, Moon," she said.

I did.

"What's going on?" I knew the twins were okay. The neighbors knew the twins were okay as loud as they were yelling.

"Honey, my sweet boy," she said. "Sometimes there are things that happen and we don't know why."

"Okay." I didn't know if I should say anything or just listen.

"Moon," she said. "Aaron Decker is in the hospital."

It was then I saw the red under her eyes from crying.

"What do you mean?" I said.

"He had an accident, sweetie. He got hurt pretty badly."

The cold returned to my body and at the same

time I started sweating. Another shiver went down my back.

"What happened?" I said.

She looked at me, her eyes moving around me quickly. "I'm not sure, Moon. I just know he's hurt. His leg is broken and I think he hit his head."

But I could tell she knew more. She just didn't want to tell me. Mom had never been good at keeping secrets, though usually it was about a family vacation to Disneyland or something fun like that.

"Does he have a concussion?" I said.

The smile she was forcing turned into a frown the moment I said it and she began crying harder as she nodded.

I watch football on Sundays with Dad and they're always talking about concussion protocol when a player gets hit in the head too hard. They have to go into a little tent and have tests done before they can play again. I doubt they took Aaron into a tent.

"Mom." My voice was so quiet I wasn't sure she could hear. But she turned her face to look at me. "Mom, I don't think it was an accident."

Her eyebrows squeezed together like they did when she was confused or curious.

"What do you mean, Moon?" she said.

I was fiddling with my fingers. She reached over and put her hands on top of mine.

This was the reason I sped home, why I rushed here to talk to her. But it was too late. It had already happened again.

"I think Aaron's dad hurts him," I said. "Like, on purpose."

I felt her shake through her hands on mine. It was the slightest vibration, so small even my seismometer couldn't have detected it, but I felt it.

I told her everything I knew, or what I thought I knew, at least. About the bruises and the broken arm. About seeing his dad shove him through the door. About Aaron walking home alone after the soccer game. Nothing seemed too small to mention. Everything felt important in that moment.

She listened quietly. Somehow we weren't interrupted by the the twins. When I was done I saw she was crying again.

"I know, Mo," she said. "I know."

"What?"

"I tried to help him," she said. "I saw the bruises on his shoulder and how he looked in pain picking up his backpack. I went with him to the counselor's office, but he just kept saying he'd had a bicycle accident."

I thought of the day in the office and seeing the counselor's door closed. She really had tried.

"Why didn't you tell me?" I said.

"I couldn't, Mo," she said. "I still probably shouldn't, but you know now. You saw it. You figured it out."

"I don't understand why his dad would hurt him," I said. "Why would a dad do that?"

She shook her head, still crying.

"I don't know, sweetie. I really don't know."

I stood up and put my arms around her and she hugged me tight. We were both crying. I heard the twins upstairs and could tell they were in my room and I didn't care.

"Mom," I said. "Can we go to the hospital?"

CHAPTER 35

I've been in a hospital exactly three times in my life. The first was when I was born. The second was when the twins were born. And the third was when Dad got his appendix out. I was young when that happened, but I remember lying on the bed with him watching *Jeopardy* on the television that hung off the ceiling. I thought that was so cool. We'd eaten a dozen tiny containers of orange Jell-O between the two of us.

Mom had made a couple of calls, then we dropped the twins off with friends down the street and drove across town. The hospital was bigger than I remembered and we probably walked at least five miles until we found a room in the pediatric section. That's where they keep the kids.

A nurse told us we weren't allowed in because we weren't family. Mom went and talked to a woman I found out was Aaron's mother. She was small and shy-looking with hair that covered her face a little. She stood with her shoulders rolled forward and it made her look smaller than she really was. While Mom was talking to her, she looked over at me and smiled.

There was a man in a suit beside her asking her questions as soon as Mom walked away. He was writing things in a notebook like the one Dad writes his songs in, but I don't think that's what this guy was doing.

"Mo, Aaron's mother said you can go in for a few minutes," she said.

I nodded. "Okay," I said. But I wasn't sure I was okay. All of a sudden I felt I shouldn't be there. I felt like I was trespassing into someone else's life.

"It's fine, Moon," Mom said. "He needs to see a friendly face right now."

Even if it's one he's tried to punch? I thought.

The door was propped open and I walked in. There were two beds, but the other one was empty. Aaron was in the one closest to the window. He was looking out at a helicopter as it flew past to land somewhere near the hospital.

"Hey, Aaron," I said.

He turned and looked at me. I half expected him to jump up and hit me. But he didn't. There was a tube running to his arm that probably kept him from doing it.

"What do you want, runt?" he said.

I really wasn't sure.

"I wanted to see how you're doing," I said.

"Well, I'm hurt. I'm sure you're happy about that."

"No," I said. "There's no way I could be happy about anyone getting hurt."

He was staring at me like I was speaking a foreign language.

"And nobody deserves to be hurt like you were," I said.

He grunted. "What do you think you know about it with your perfect little house and perfect little family?"

"I know I've tried several times to be your friend. I didn't want you hitting me, but I also didn't want you walking to soccer practice alone and feeling like you couldn't talk to anyone."

"Whatever." He turned back to the window.

I felt safe, for some reason. Maybe because he had a broken leg and couldn't chase me, or the

IV coming out of his arm. But I really think it was because I knew his secret now. Whether he liked it or not, we were connected.

"When you come back to soccer practice, I'm going to keep trying to talk to you," I said. "And when school starts, I'll keep trying to talk to you."

He didn't move.

"You can push me and punch me and bloody my nose if you want, but I'm going to keep trying. We don't have to be best friends," I said. "But we can be friendly. I already have a best friend. His name is Felix and I think you'd like him. We play soccer in his backyard. You could come play with us sometime. It's the big stone house two down from mine."

Aaron turned his head back and looked at me.

"Why are you doing this," he said.

I thought about it for a moment.

"I don't know," I said. "I guess I just think everyone should have a friend."

CHAPTER 36

The world seemed a lot bigger than it had. There was so much I didn't know, which makes sense since I'm only a kid. Sure, in the fall I'd be in the sixth grade. Top class at Tall Pines Elementary. But that didn't seem important anymore.

I let Dad drive me to soccer practice because I knew he enjoyed it. I also didn't feel like being alone. Since leaving the hospital the day before, I stayed in my room a lot. I pretended to read some books. Played a few video games, but wasn't paying attention and lost. Nothing felt important enough compared to what I'd seen.

I knew Aaron wouldn't be at soccer because of his leg. I thought about asking Mom to take me to see him again tomorrow, but he'd left the hospital and I didn't really want to go into his house. Not alone, at least.

When all the boys arrived, the coach called us into a group.

"We're a man down," he said. "Aaron Decker isn't on the team anymore. We'll try to get someone to replace him, but until then we all have to work extra hard."

I heard everything he said and none of it made sense. Why was Aaron not playing anymore? Was he upset that I said I'd keep talking to him? I knew he needed time to heal, but he didn't have to quit.

Practice began and we were running drills through the cones, kicking goals, and all the usual stuff. During water breaks some of the boys were joking around and wrestling and squirting water on each other.

It was just like any normal practice.

But it didn't feel like one to me. It seemed unimportant and more important at the same time. It was just a game but we were lucky to be out here, to get to play soccer, *the beautiful game* as Coach said.

Dad sat on the bench on the far side of the field. He was writing in his notebook again. A few other parents were talking and their laughter would float across the green turf.

It was all normal and it shouldn't be.

Didn't they know what happened? Didn't they care?

After Coach released us, I went over to where Dad was and sat next to him.

"Ready to go, son?" he said.

"Not yet," I said.

The lights made the green of the field glow. It was beautiful in its own way. I waited so long to be on a soccer team, to play on these fields.

"How can things go on like they were?" I said.

He closed his notebook and put it in the pocket of his khakis.

"Why is nothing different? Am I the only one that cares?" I said.

"No. You definitely aren't the only one who cares, Moon," he said. "Not everyone knows what we know. And even if they did, the world has to keep spinning. People have to go to work. Kids have to go to soccer practice."

"Aaron doesn't," I said. "He quit the team."

"I don't have all the answers for you, Moon. I really wish I did. But don't for a second think things aren't different. More people know about Aaron now, and that means there are more people to help him. Things will get better for him. And you learned something important about how sometimes bad things can happen in this world, and that we all have to watch out for each other."

"I guess," I said.

"You were so brave going to Mom to tell her," he said. "And you cared enough to notice what was happening to him, even though he was mean to you. I couldn't be more proud of you, Moon."

The lights on the fields started going off one at a time until the ones over us went dark with a huge thudding noise. The darkness felt good. It felt comfortable.

"Dad," I said.

"What, son?"

"I really liked your song about me."

CHAPTER 37

Another soccer game came and went. We lost 2-to-1. Coach said we played well but I don't know how that's true if we didn't win.

I was kicking the ball with Felix in his back yard after the game. He was telling me about things he'd been doing with his homeschool friends. It was the reverse of how it used to be, me rushing over to tell him about a day in school.

There's a lot of summer left. A lot of soccer. A lot of afternoons hanging out with Felix and Debbie. The three of us are going to play mini-golf next weekend.

I kicked the ball back to Felix and he stopped talking in the middle of a word. The ball rolled right past him into a holly bush. I thought he was staring at me then I realized he was staring behind me.

I turned around.

Aaron Decker was standing there. He had a pair of metal crutches. His left leg was in a cast and there were still some bruises on his forehead.

I hadn't told Felix anything about what happened to Aaron. It wasn't my story to tell.

"Hey," I said.

"Hey," Aaron said.

I was pretty sure he wasn't there to push me or punch me.

"So you aren't playing soccer anymore?" I said.

"Nah," he said. "I'm not gonna be around."

"Where are you going?"

He looked over his shoulder to the street. A brown four-door car was sitting at the curb. I could see his mom in the driver's seat. The back seat was full of boxes.

"My mom and I are going to stay at my grandparents' place for a while," he said. "They live like an hour from here."

I nodded, not knowing what else to say.

"Well, I wanted to…" His voice faded off. He looked down at the ground and kicked at a rock that wasn't there. "Wanted to say I'm sorry for how I treated you."

"It's okay," I said.

"It isn't. I was just…it wasn't fair. You seem like a good guy."

"Thanks."

Felix came closer and was just behind me.

"This is my best friend Felix," I said. "I was telling you about him in the hos— I told you about him."

"Hey, Felix," Aaron said.

"Hi."

I looked down at his cast. It was still mostly white but fading with dirt a little. There was no writing on it.

"Can I sign your cast?" I said.

I thought I saw a hint of a smile.

"Sure. You got a pen?"

"I'll get one," Felix said. He ran through the back door of his house.

There was only a few moments I'd be totally alone with Aaron Decker, and probably for the last time. I didn't want to push my luck, but also believed I should.

"I'm really sorry about what happened to you. That's what isn't fair," I said. "You seem like a good guy, too."

Felix was back with a black marker before Aaron could respond. But he hadn't punched me or hit me with one of his crutches, so I took that as a good sign.

Aaron sat down on the picnic table bench and I kneeled down. With the marker I wrote a short message.

"Can I sign it, too?" Felix said. "I've never signed a cast."

Aaron actually laughed a little and I realized I'd never heard him laugh. "Sure. Have at it."

While Felix was kneeling down writing on the cast, I just looked at Aaron for a second. He looked back at me. It was the first time we'd made eye contact, I'm pretty sure. But what I'd seen of him at a distance, he seemed different now. He always looked a little, I don't know, lost maybe.

But today there was something else. Something a little better. More hopeful, maybe.

Felix finished and stood. Aaron looked down at the messages and saw mine.

"What is that?" He said.

"It's my email address," I said. "In case you ever want to talk or something."

It was then that I knew that I no longer had an enemy. I didn't have a bully tormenting me anymore. I saw this huge boy towering over me. He turned his head away, pretending to look over at his mom's car again, but I saw the smallest bit of moisture in his eyes.

"Thanks, Mo," he said.

"Nah. That doesn't feel right." I shook my head. "Call me Runt."

CHAPTER 38

I've been called a lot of things.

Mo.
Shorty.
Mini Mo.
Bilbo Baggins.
Yoda's smaller brother.
Runt.

But I'm Moon Noonan. And that's the name I asked the teachers to call me on the first day of sixth grade at Tall Pines Elementary.

And after a long summer of fighting with his parents about it, my best friend Felix is back in school with me. The two musketeers. He of course brings his own lunch, carries an inhaler everywhere, and his parents have spoken to all of the teachers in the building to make sure they know how sensitive he is to, well, everything.

It's our last year in the school. Top dogs. The upperclassmen of the lowest grades.

I'm still the shortest guy in my class, but I don't care. Half of the fifth graders are taller than me now. Size is just a state of mind, my dad would tell me, and I finally understood that.

My soccer team won most of our games and lost in the finals. So we were the second best team in the league. I scored four more goals over the rest of the season.

The seismometer I built spent all summer in the window at Mr. Kaplan's hardware store. He actually looked sad when I picked it up. Now Dad has it on the counter at his orthodontist office. I finally moved the trophy up to my bedroom.

I got home from school on Friday at the end of the first week. Felix had to go to a doctor's appointment so I couldn't go to his place. I opened my computer to play some games and saw I had an email. It was from Aaron.

Hey, Runt.

I started at my new school this week and it's pretty good. It's not as nice as Tall Pines Elementary, but the playground is huge and there are real soccer goals.

Mom got us an apartment near my grandma's house. It's small but I have my own bedroom. And get this, my mom's gonna be a substitute teacher just like yours.

Well, I don't know what else to say, I just wanted to write. When they cut my cast off, I had them keep the part with your email address on it.

Oh, I'm sending you a picture of me and my new friend here. His name is Calvin but he goes by Cal.

Later.
Aaron

I scrolled down and saw the picture. It was Aaron standing next to another boy that was a lot shorter than him. Like my height. They're standing on a soccer field and wearing matching blue jerseys.

Aaron is smiling.

ABOUT THE AUTHOR

John H. Matthews loved to read when he was a kid. *Bridge to Terabithia*, by Katherine Paterson, is his favorite from when he was young. Now he gets to read so many wonderful books with his son. Some of his favorites from now are *Crenshaw*, by Katherine Applegate, and *Hello, Universe*, by Erin Entrada Kelly.

He has lived all over the United States, but now resides in the Washington, D.C. suburbs of Fairfax, Virginia, with his wife and nine year old son, Brennan. He spends his time working, writing, and watching soccer and tennis practices.

While he has been writing books for grownups for several years, he wanted to write something his son could read and enjoy, hopefully for years to come.

www.jhmatthews.com

ACKNOWLEDGEMENTS

I am so fortunate to have had so many wonderful people to talk to while writing this book, and to read it once it was done, including several parents, a child psychologist, an elementary school teacher, two school nurses, a pediatrician, and the kids this book is for. Thank you all so much for your help!

Shea Megale, my incredible friend and editor, thank you for your sharp eye, blunt critique, and everlasting support.

Ed Hutchison, you have helped make my last several books as close to perfect as they can be. Thank you for taking so much of your own time for me.

And Sara Willia, your illustrations take this book over the top. They are perfect. I can't wait to work with you again!

THE KIDS

Carson Stuckey

Keira Farrell

Kylee Farrell

Christopher Lindlau

Ella Matterazzo

James Matterazzo

Brennan Matthews

THE GROWNUPS

Wyatt Akins

Tracy Brown

Melinda Harris Brownell

Elizabeth Harvey

Ed Hutchison

Shea Megale

Kristine Farrell

Hung Le

Jeff and Dana Su Lindlau

Amy Applegate Matterazzo

Windi Oehms

Amy Pettie

Stephanie Sniffin

Sara Willia

A NOTE FROM MOON

I saw what was happening to Aaron and didn't understand it. My mom and dad love me. It's their job to take care of me and keep me safe. But I learned a lot from Aaron. I learned that kids need to watch out for each other, whether it's from bullies or grown ups.

There's things we can do to help. Or if it is happening to you, things you can do to help yourself.

If you think a kid is being hurt by a grownup, or by another kid, tell a safe adult. A safe adult could be your teacher, your school counselor, or your mom and dad. Anyone you trust. The sooner you tell them, the better.

If you are being hurt by someone, tell a safe adult as soon as possible. It can be your aunt or uncle or grandparents in another state, or your teacher, school counselor or principal. If you don't have anyone to tell, there is a phone number you can call or even text. It's that easy. Even kids like us can do it.

The **Childhelp National Child Abuse Hotline** has counselors (that's a safe adult) available all day and night, every day, in a ton of different languages. Call or text **1-800-4-A-CHILD** (1-800-422-4453) or go to the website at www. childhelp.org/hotline.

If you or someone you know is being bullied, you can find stuff out about it at www. stopbullying.gov.

I'm off to play with Felix now. He's finally going to try out for the soccer team next summer!

- Moon Noonan

And don't forget...
everyone can use a friend.

Made in the USA
Middletown, DE
17 May 2021

39932771R00118